DESSERTS

by
Jean Paré

Dedication

Time for something sinful!

Cover Photo
Bocconne Dolce page 97

DESSERTS

Copyright © 1986 by Company's Coming Publishing Limited
All Rights Reserved

Seventeenth Printing August 1996

ISBN 0-9690695-5-3

Published and Distributed by
Company's Coming Publishing Limited
Box 8037, Station "F"
Edmonton, Alberta, Canada
T6H 4N9

**Published Simultaneously in
Canada and the United States of America**

Printed In Canada

Company's Coming Cookbooks by Jean Paré

COMPANY'S COMING SERIES
English

- 150 DELICIOUS SQUARES
- CASSEROLES
- MUFFINS & MORE
- SALADS
- APPETIZERS
- DESSERTS
- SOUPS & SANDWICHES
- HOLIDAY ENTERTAINING
- COOKIES
- VEGETABLES
- MAIN COURSES
- PASTA
- CAKES
- BARBECUES
- DINNERS OF THE WORLD
- LUNCHES
- PIES
- LIGHT RECIPES
- MICROWAVE COOKING
- PRESERVES
- LIGHT CASSEROLES
- CHICKEN, ETC.
- KIDS COOKING
- FISH & SEAFOOD
- BREADS
- MEATLESS COOKING (April 1997)

PINT SIZE BOOKS
English

- FINGER FOOD
- PARTY PLANNING
- BUFFETS
- BAKING DELIGHTS
- CHOCOLATE

JEAN PARÉ LIVRES DE CUISINE
French

- 150 DÉLICIEUX CARRÉS
- LES CASSEROLES
- MUFFINS ET PLUS
- LES DÎNERS
- LES BARBECUES
- LES TARTES
- DÉLICES DES FÊTES
- RECETTES LÉGÈRES
- LES SALADES
- LA CUISSON AU MICRO-ONDES
- LES PÂTES
- LES CONSERVES
- LES CASSEROLES LÉGÈRES
- POULET, ETC.
- LA CUISINE POUR LES ENFANTS
- POISSONS ET FRUITS DE MER
- LES PAINS
- LA CUISINE SANS VIANDE (avril 1997)

table of Contents

The Jean Paré Story	6
Foreword	7
Cake-Type Desserts	9
Cheesecakes	29
Chilled Desserts	40
Frozen Desserts	70
Fruit Desserts	81
Meringue-Type Desserts	91
Pastry	98
Puddings	111
Sauces	136
Special Drinks And Confections	145
Measurement Tables	150
Index	151
Mail Order Form	157

the Jean Paré story

Jean Paré grew up understanding that the combination of family, friends and home cooking is the essence of a good life. From her mother she learned to appreciate good cooking, while her father praised even her earliest attempts. When she left home she took with her many acquired family recipes, her love of cooking and her intriguing desire to read recipe books like novels!

In 1963, when her four children had all reached school age, Jean volunteered to cater to the 50th anniversary of the Vermilion School of Agriculture, now Lakeland College. Working out of her home, Jean prepared a dinner for over 1000 people which launched a flourishing catering operation that continued for over eighteen years. During that time she was provided with countless opportunities to test new ideas with immediate feedback—resulting in empty plates and contented customers! Whether preparing cocktail sandwiches for a house party or serving a hot meal for 1500 people, Jean Paré earned a reputation for good food, courteous service and reasonable prices.

"Why don't you write a cookbook?" Time and again, as requests for her recipes mounted, Jean was asked that question. Jean's response was to team up with her son, Grant Lovig, in the fall of 1980 to form Company's Coming Publishing Limited. April 14, 1981, marked the debut of "150 DELICIOUS SQUARES", the first Company's Coming cookbook in what soon would become Canada's most popular cookbook series. By 1995, sales had surpassed ten million cookbooks.

Jean Paré's operation has grown from the early days of working out of a spare bedroom in her home to operating a large and fully equipped test kitchen in Vermilion, Alberta, near the home she and her husband Larry built. Full-time staff has grown steadily to include marketing personnel located in major cities across Canada plus selected U.S. markets. Home Office is located in Edmonton, Alberta where distribution, accounting and administration functions are headquartered in the company's own 20,000 square foot facility. Growth continues with the recent addition of the Recipe Factory, a 2700 square foot test kitchen and photography studio located in Edmonton.

Company's Coming cookbooks are now distributed throughout Canada and the United States plus numerous overseas markets, all under the guidance of Jean's daughter, Gail Lovig. The series is published in English and French, plus a Spanish language edition is available in Mexico. Soon the familiar and trusted Company's Coming style of recipes will be available in a variety of formats in addition to the bestselling soft cover series.

Jean Paré's approach to cooking has always called for quick and easy recipes using everyday ingredients. She continues to gain new supporters by adhering to what she calls "the golden rule of cooking": never share a recipe you wouldn't use yourself. It's an approach that works—*ten million times over!*

Foreword

If it is true that the last word spoken is most often the first remembered, one can readily appreciate the importance of a good dessert. Whether served as a grand finale to a satisfying meal or simply on its own with a hot or cold beverage, dessert sets no limit on your creativity.

Should you wish to compensate for serving a light meal, a richer, more elaborate dessert could follow. Some favorites are Apple Pan Dowdy, Lemon Cheesecake or Cloud Nine. Following a heavier meal or for a light snack, you might choose Crème Caramel, Fruit Pizza or Cream Puffs. Serving a variety of desserts is a sure way to impress when company's coming.

Puddings are not only economical but are enjoying a resurgence in popularity as cooks continue their search for home-made goodness. Try Quick Apple Pudding, Blueberry Grunt or Brown Betty and you will understand why.

Some types of desserts tend to overlap. For example, some cheesecakes are unbaked as are chilled desserts. Meanwhile, some chilled desserts contain cream cheese but are not commonly known as cheesecakes. The index is cross referenced for your convenience.

For the last word in entertaining, read on and enjoy desserts!

Jean Paré

GINGERBREAD

An easy one-bowl method. Enjoy it hot with a sauce and cold as a Baked Alaska.

All-purpose flour	2 cups	500 mL
Granulated sugar	½ cup	125 mL
Butter or Margarine	½ cup	125 mL
Cinnamon	1 tsp.	5 mL
Allspice	1 tsp.	5 mL
Ginger	1 tsp.	5 mL
Salt	¼ tsp.	1 mL
Molasses (mild)	1 cup	250 mL
Eggs	3	3
Cooking oil	¼ cup	60 mL
Hot water	1 cup	250 mL
Baking soda	2 tsp.	10 mL

Measure first 9 ingredients into mixing bowl.

Measure hot water. Stir in baking soda. Add to first 8 ingredients and beat until mixed well. Pour into greased 9 x 13 inch (22 x 33 cm) pan. Bake in 350°F (180°C) oven for 35 to 40 minutes or until an inserted toothpick comes out clean. Serve warm with whipped cream, Lemon Sauce, page 141, or Brown Sugar Sauce, page 142. Makes 15 servings.

AN ANGEL'S CAKE

So delicate looking — like a rainbow.

Large angel food cake, tinted green	1	1
Large angel food cake, white	1	1
Lemon pie fillings (not instant), enough for 2 pies	2	2

Brush brown crumbs off cakes. Cut both cakes with serrated knife into small chunks.

Cook lemon pie fillings according to package directions. Cool.

Cover bottom of tube pan with waxed paper. Cover with a thin layer of lemon filling. Drop in ⅓ of cake pieces, alternating colors. Spoon lemon mixture over top. Put remaining cake pieces on top, ⅓ each time, covering with lemon mixture. Chill. Unmold to serve. Cuts into 16 pieces.

Pictured on page 17.

BLACK FOREST CAKE

This version is quick and easy without sacrificing flavor. Impress your friends.

Dark chocolate cake layers, 8 or 9-inch (20 or 23 cm) round	2	2
Kirsch — a generous sprinkling (or sherry or fruit juice)		
Icing (confectioner's) sugar	1 cup	250 mL
Cocoa	2 tbsp.	30 mL
Butter or margarine	2 tbsp.	30 mL
Prepared coffee or water	1 tbsp.	15 mL
Can of cherry pie filling	19 oz.	540 mL
Whipping cream (or 1½ env. topping)	1½ cups	375 mL
Granulated sugar	4 tsp.	20 mL
Vanilla	1 tsp.	5 mL

First make icing. Beat icing sugar, cocoa, butter and coffee or water together adding a bit more liquid if needed.

To assemble cake, put 1 layer on cake plate, rounded side down. Sprinkle generously with kirsch. Apply ½ of chocolate icing to top of layer on the outside edge only, forming a rim about ½ inch (1.25 cm) high and ¾ inch (2 cm) wide. Spread ½ can cherry pie filling over layer keeping it inside of icing rim. Put second layer, flat side down, over top. Sprinkle with kirsch. Cut rounded top off if needed to make top flat enough so that cherries will stay in place. Make another icing rim. Spread second ½ can cherry pie filling over top, keeping inside of rim.

Whip cream, sugar and vanilla until stiff. Using rubber spatula, ice sides of cake with whipped cream. Pile rest of cream on top center of cake. Spread almost to edge of cherries so some cherries may still be seen or leave some center cherries showing and spread cream around the top edges. Top with stemmed cherries and/or chocolate curls to make it extra special. Slice into 12 generous portions.

Variation: Canned black cherries, pitted, may be used. Thicken juice of 2-14 oz. (2-398 mL) cans with 2 tbsp. (30 mL) cornstarch stirred into juice, then heat and stir to boil and thicken.

BLACK FOREST BOWL: Partly fill bowl with chunks of chocolate cake. Spoon cherry pie filling over top. Put sweetened whipped cream over all. Garnish with shaved chocolate and cherries. Chill.

CHOCOLATE ANGEL CAKE

Cutting into this dessert exposes a chocolate filled tunnel.

Large angel food cake	1	1
Whipping cream (or 3 env. topping)	3 cups	750 mL
Icing (confectioner's) sugar	1½ cups	375 mL
Cocoa	¾ cup	175 mL
Rum flavoring (optional, but good)	1 tsp.	5 mL

Slice layer 1 inch (2.5 cm) thick from top of cake. Set aside. Remove cake to form a tunnel leaving walls and bottom 1 inch (2.5 cm) thick. Cut removed cake into chunks.

Beat cream, sugar, cocoa and flavoring together until stiff. In another bowl, fold about ⅓ whipped cream mixture with cake chunks. Spoon into tunnel. Replace top layer. Frost with remaining ⅔ cream mixture. Chill. Cuts into 16 slices.

RASPBERRY TUNNEL: Add ½ cup (125 mL) fresh raspberries to 1 cup (250 mL) whipping cream. Beat together until stiff. Fold cake pieces into cream. Stuff tunnel and replace top. Serve with or without whipped cream and raspberries as a garnish.

BISCUIT SHORTCAKE

To some, a biscuit type cake is a true shortcake. To others a layer cake is a must. This is a biscuit type that is sure to please.

All-purpose flour	2 cups	500 mL
Granulated sugar	¼ cup	50 mL
Baking powder	4 tsp.	20 mL
Salt	½ tsp.	2 mL
Cold butter or margarine	¼ cup	50 mL
Egg	1	1
Milk	⅔ cup	150 mL

In large bowl put flour, sugar, baking powder and salt. Add butter. Cut in until crumbly. Make a well in center.

In small bowl beat egg until frothy. Stir in milk. Pour into well. Stir with a fork to form soft dough. Turn out on lightly floured surface. Knead 8-10 times. Press into 2 greased 8-inch (20 cm) layer pans. Bake in 425°F (220°C) oven for 15 minutes until risen and browned slightly. Cool. Fill with sweetened fruit and top with more sweetened fruit and whipped cream. For single serving size, cut 1 inch (2.5 cm) thick dough into 3-inch (7.5 cm) circles. Bake. Cool and split to use as layers.

STRAWBERRY SHORTCAKE

A summer classic that is good any time of year.

White layer cake, or Biscuit Shortcake, your own or a mix (see page 11)	1	1
Fresh strawberries	2 pts.	1 L
Granulated sugar to taste	2 – 3 tbsp.	30 – 50 mL
Whipping cream (or 1 env. topping)	1 cup	250 mL
Granulated sugar	1 tbsp.	15 mL
Vanilla	½ tsp.	2 mL

Place one layer of cake, flat side up, on serving plate.

Mash strawberries, adding sugar to taste. Spread ½ of the berries over cake layer. Place second layer, flat side down, over top. Spread second ½ of berries over the top layer. Cover and refrigerate until ready to serve.

Put cream, sugar and vanilla into bowl. Beat until stiff. Spread over the top layer of strawberries. Cut into wedges to serve. Serves 12.

RASPBERRY SHORTCAKE: Use fresh raspberries instead of straw‑berries.

PEACH SHORTCAKE: Use fresh peaches, mashed or sliced, instead of strawberries.

Jail buddies are better known as pen pals.

PINEAPPLE UPSIDE DOWN CAKE

A favorite for pineapple lovers. Try making your own pineapple and pecan design on the pan bottom.

Butter or margarine	3 tbsp.	50 mL
Brown sugar, packed	½ cup	125 mL
Pineapple rings, drained	19 oz.	540 mL
Red maraschino cherries	9	9
Butter or margarine, softened	⅓ cup	75 mL
Granulated sugar	¾ cup	175 mL
Egg	1	1
All-purpose flour	1½ cups	350 mL
Baking powder	2 tsp.	10 mL
Salt	¼ tsp.	1 mL
Milk	⅔ cup	150 mL
Vanilla	1 tsp.	5 mL

Melt butter in 9 x 9-inch (22 x 22 cm) pan. Stir in brown sugar. Arrange pineapple rings over top. Place 1 cherry in center of each ring.

Measure next 8 ingredients into mixing bowl. Beat on low speed to combine. Beat on medium speed for 2 minutes. Batter will be thick. Spoon over pineapple. Bake in 350°F (180°C) oven for 40 to 50 minutes until an inserted toothpick comes out clean. Let stand 5 minutes. Invert onto plate or small tray. Remove pan. Cool. Serve with whipped cream or just cream. Cuts into 9 servings.

Variation: Use crushed pineapple, drained, instead of rings. Cherries may be omitted.

PEACH UPSIDE DOWN CAKE: Use sliced peaches, drained, instead of pineapple rings.

TUNNEL OF PEACHES

A light, tasty and pretty dessert.

Large baked angel food cake	1	1
Vanilla pudding and pie filling, 4 serving size	1	1
Milk	2 cups	450 mL
Whipping cream (or 1 env. topping)	1 cup	250 mL
Almond flavoring	½ tsp.	2 mL
Can of sliced peaches, drained	14 oz.	398 mL

Cut a 1 inch (2.5 cm) thick layer from top of cake. Set aside. Hollow out cake leaving inside and outside walls, as well as the bottom, 1 inch (2.5 cm) thick. Cut removed cake into small chunks. Set aside.

Cook pudding and milk according to directions on package. Chill thoroughly.

Beat cream and almond until thick. Fold into cooled pudding. Add removed cake chunks and sliced peaches. Fold in. Spoon into tunnel. Place removed layer on top. May be iced with 1 cup (250 mL) additional cream, whipped, or served plain. Makes 16 slices.

PEACH FILLED ANGEL CAKE: Omit peaches and fold in ½ of 19 oz. (540 mL) peach pie filling. Add other ½ can to 1½–2 cups (375–500 mL) cream, whipped. Use this to frost cake.

Is it proper to say "Hail to the Queen" when she's reigning?

STRAWBERRY ANGEL DESSERT

This tastes just as good as it looks. An absolute delight!

Frozen strawberries, thawed, drained, juice reserved	15 oz.	425 g
Strawberry flavored gelatin	3 oz.	85 g
Boiling water	1 cup	250 mL
Granulated sugar	½ cup	125 mL
Reserved strawberry juice plus water, if needed, to make	1 cup	200 mL
Large angel food cake	1	1
Whipping cream (or 1 env. topping)	1 cup	250 mL
Granulated sugar	1 tbsp.	15 mL
Vanilla	½ tsp.	2 mL

Dissolve gelatin in boiling water. Stir in sugar and strawberry juice. Chill until syrupy.

Break cake into small pieces. Layer ½ in ungreased 9 x 13-inch (22 x 33 cm) pan. Fold strawberries into jelly mixture. Spoon ½ over cake in pan. Spread remaining cake over top. Cover with remaining jelly mixture. Chill.

To serve, whip cream, sugar and vanilla until stiff. Spread over all or put a dollop on each piece. Cuts into 15 pieces.

STRAWBERRY TUNNEL: Cut 1-inch (2.5 cm) layer from top of cake. Hollow out cake leaving sides and bottom 1 inch (2.5 cm) thick. Fill with strawberry cake mixture. Replace top layer. Tint whipped cream pink, then frost.

RASPBERRY ANGEL DESSERT: Substitute frozen raspberries for strawberries.

ORANGE ANGEL DESSERT

Light and delicate.

Vanilla ice cream	1 pt.	500 mL
Lemon flavored gelatin	3 oz.	85 g
Boiling water	1 cup	250 mL
Can of frozen orange juice	6¼ oz.	178 mL
Angel food cake	1	1

Remove ice cream from freezer to soften.

In medium-size bowl, dissolve gelatin in boiling water. Stir in frozen orange juice. Chill until syrupy.

Fold softened ice cream into thickened jelly. Cut cake with serrated knife into small pieces. Arrange about ½ cake pieces in ungreased 9 x 13-inch (22 x 33 cm) pan. Spoon on ½ orange mixture. Cover with second ½ cake pieces. Top with second ½ orange mixture. Chill. Cuts into 12–15 pieces.

1. Blitz Torte page 21.
2. An Angel's Cake page 9.
3. Pumpkin Jelly Roll page 25.

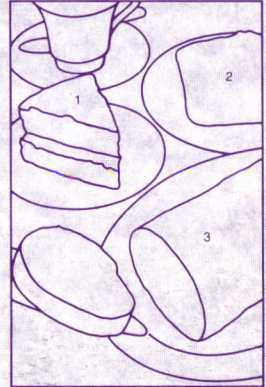

ANGEL FOOD CAKE

A make-it-from-scratch cake. In countries where this is unknown, it may be baked in some smaller pans. It can then be cut up and used in the several recipes in this book requiring Angel Food cake. Plain white cake may be substituted but there is quite a difference.

Sifted cake flour	1 cup	250 mL
Granulated sugar	½ cup	125 mL
Egg whites, at least 2 days old (about 8–12) room temperature	1¼ cups	300 mL
Cream of tartar	1¼ tsp.	6 mL
Salt	¼ tsp.	1 mL
Vanilla	1 tsp.	5 mL
Almond flavoring	¼ tsp.	1 mL
Granulated sugar	1 cup	250 mL

Sift cake flour. Measure required amount. Sift flour and sugar together 3 times. Use 2 pieces of waxed paper to sift onto.

Beat egg whites until frothy. Add cream of tartar, salt, vanilla and almond flavoring. Beat until soft peaks form.

Add 1 cup (250 mL) sugar 1 tbsp. (15 mL) at a time, continuing to beat until it is all added and whites stand in stiff peaks. Fold in ¼ flour mixture at a time. Turn into ungreased 10-inch (25 cm) tube pan. Gently cut through batter with knife to remove air pockets. Bake in 375°F (190°C) oven for about 35 minutes. It will spring back when touched or test with pick. Invert pan to cool. Rest tube over neck of bottle or funnel or rest pan edges on racks.

Note: For slightly more volume, use 1½ cups (375 mL) egg whites and 1½ tsp. (7 mL) cream of tartar.

SACHER TORTE

A good replica of the original from the Hotel Sacher in Vienna.

Butter or margarine	½ cup	125 mL
Granulated sugar	¾ cup	175 mL
Semisweet chocolate chips, melted	1 cup	250 mL
Vanilla	1 tsp.	5 mL
Egg yolks	6	6
All-purpose flour	¾ cup	175 mL
Egg whites, room temperature	6	6

Cream butter and sugar together well.

Slowly beat in melted chocolate and vanilla. Add egg yolks, 1 at a time, beating after each addition. Stir in flour.

Beat egg whites until stiff. Fold into batter. Spoon into a greased 9-inch (22 cm) round layer pan. Bake in 350°F (180°C) oven for about 35 minutes or until an inserted toothpick comes out clean. Cool 10 minutes. Turn cake out on rack. Cool. Place on flat plate, round side up. Glaze with apricot jam and icing. Cake may be sliced into 2 layers. In that case, increase jam to 6 tbsp. (90 mL) and spread between layers, on top layer and sides. Glaze with chocolate.

TOPPING

Apricot jam, sieved	4 tbsp.	50 mL
Semisweet chocolate chips	½ cup	125 mL
Evaporated milk	3 tbsp.	50 mL

Spread jam over top of cake.

Melt chips and milk in saucepan over medium heat. Cool to lukewarm. Spread over top and sides of cake.

BLITZ TORTE

This Swedish delight will become one of your favorites. It looks complicated but is easy to make.

Butter or margarine	½ cup	125 mL
Granulated sugar	¾ cup	175 mL
Egg yolks	4	4
Milk	5 tbsp.	75 mL
All-purpose flour	1 cup	250 mL
Baking powder	1 tsp.	5 mL
Vanilla	1 tsp.	5 mL
Egg whites, room temperature	4	4
Cream of tartar	¼ tsp.	1 mL
Granulated sugar	¾ cup	175 mL
Finely chopped nuts	¾ cup	175 mL

FILLING

Vanilla pudding and pie filling, 4 serving size, cooked (or make your own custard)	1	1

Cream butter and first amount of sugar. Beat in egg yolks and milk. Stir in flour, baking powder and vanilla. Spread into 2 greased 9-inch (22 cm) layer pans. Set aside.

Beat egg whites and cream of tartar until soft peaks form. Gradually add second amount of sugar, beating until stiff. Fold in nuts. Spread over batter in pans. Bake in 325°F (160°C) oven for 40 minutes.

Filling: Cook pudding according to package directions. Cool. Assemble as for layer cake, using custard between layers. Sides of cake may be frosted with whipped cream if desired. Bottom layer may be turned meringue side up or down, although it will stick to plate if turned down.

Pictured on page 17.

Growing older is like making a pudding. You get lumps if you don't stir.

JELLY ROLL

This light roll is always popular. Whether you choose jam, lemon filling or even pie filling or ice cream, it will disappear in a hurry.

Eggs, room temperature	4	4
Granulated sugar	1 cup	250 mL
Water	¼ cup	60 mL
Vanilla	1 tsp.	5 mL
All-purpose flour	1 cup	250 mL
Baking powder	2 tsp.	10 mL
Salt	¼ tsp.	1 mL
Icing (confectioner's) sugar		

Grease 10 x 15-inch (25 x 38 cm) jelly roll pan. Line with waxed paper.

Beat eggs in mixing bowl until frothy. Add sugar and beat until light colored and thick. Mix in water and vanilla.

Sift flour, baking powder and salt over egg mixture and fold in.

Turn into prepared pan. Bake in 400°F (200°C) oven for 12 to 15 minutes until an inserted toothpick comes out clean. Sift icing (confectioner's) sugar over tea towel. Turn cake out onto sugar. Peel off waxed paper. Trim crisp edges if any. Roll from narrow end, towel and cake together. Cool. Unroll. Fill with filling. Reroll.

RASPBERRY FILLING: Working quickly, raspberry jam can be spread over cake as soon as paper is peeled off. Roll cake, cover with towel and cool. Saves rerolling.

LEMON FILLING

Water	2 cups	500 mL
Cornstarch	6 tbsp.	100 mL
Granulated sugar	1½ cups	375 mL
Salt	¼ tsp.	1 mL
Lemon juice	½ cup	125 mL
Eggs	2	2

Heat water in saucepan over medium heat until boiling.

Stir cornstarch, sugar and salt together in bowl. Add lemon juice and eggs. Mix well. Pour, stirring, into boiling water. Cook and stir until it thickens. Cool, then spread over cake and roll.

ICE CREAM FILLING: Slice your favorite kind about ½ inch (1 cm) thick over top. Roll. Freeze until needed.

CRANBERRY FILLING: Beat together until stiff, 1 cup (250 mL) whipping cream and 2 tbsp. (30 mL) granulated sugar until stiff. Fold in 1 cup (250 mL) whole cranberry sauce, drained a bit, and spread over cake. Roll. Chill.

STRAWBERRY CREAM: Beat 1 cup (250 mL) whipping cream and 3 tbsp. (50 mL) granulated sugar together until stiff. Spread over cake. Scatter about 2 cups (500 mL) sliced strawberries over top. Roll. Top each slice with whipped cream and a whole strawberry. This shouldn't be filled too far in advance.

PEACH CREAM: Make as for Strawberry Cream using fresh sliced or frozen peaches which have been thawed and drained. This should not be filled too far ahead.

STRAWBERRY SAUCE: Drain 15 oz. (425 g) frozen strawberries. Stir 1 tbsp. (15 mL) cornstarch into juice in saucepan. Bring to boil, stirring, until thickened. Cool. Stir in berries. Spread over cake. Roll. Serve with whipped cream.

QUICK BLACK FOREST

A snap to make with chocolate chips as an added bonus.

Devil's Food cake mix with pudding	1	1
Eggs, beaten	3	3
Almond flavoring	1 tbsp.	15 mL
Cherry pie filling	19 oz.	540 mL
Semisweet chocolate chips	1 cup	250 mL

Mix all together well with spoon. Turn into greased 9 × 13-inch (22 × 33 cm) pan. Bake in 350°F (180°C) oven for about 45 to 50 minutes or until an inserted toothpick comes out clean. Cool and glaze. Serve as is or with sweetened whipped cream, topped with a cherry. Cuts into 15 pieces.

GLAZE

Semisweet chocolate chips	½ cup	125 mL
Butter or margarine	1 tbsp.	15 mL
Milk	2 tbsp.	30 mL
Icing (confectioner's) sugar	½ cup	125 mL

Heat chips, butter and milk in saucepan over medium heat.

Stir in icing sugar. Spread over cooled cake.

CHOCOLATE ROLL

A jelly roll lined with chocolate and cream. Contains no flour. Extraordinary!

Egg whites, room temperature	6	6
Granulated sugar	¼ cup	60 mL
Egg yolks	6	6
Granulated sugar	½ cup	125 mL
Cocoa	6 tbsp.	100 mL
Vanilla	½ tsp.	2 mL

Line greased 10 x 15–inch (25 x 38 cm) jelly roll pan with waxed paper.

Beat egg whites until soft peaks form. Add sugar and beat until stiff.

Beat egg yolks with sugar until lemon colored and light. Beat in cocoa and vanilla. Fold into egg whites. Spread into prepared pan. Bake in 350°F (180°C) oven for 15 to 20 minutes until an inserted toothpick comes out clean. Sift icing (confectioner's) sugar over a tea towel. Turn cake out on top of towel. Peel off paper. Starting at narrow end, roll towel and cake up together to cool. When cool, unroll and spread filling.

FILLING

Semisweet chocolate chips	⅔ cup	150 mL
Water	2 tbsp.	30 mL
Whipping cream	1½ cups	375 mL

Melt chips and water together over hot water. Spread over cake.

Whip cream until stiff. Spread over chocolate layer, saving a bit to garnish top with a few dabs. Roll.

When a commercial painter watered down his paint, his conscience clearly said "Repaint, you thinner."

PUMPKIN JELLY ROLL

A great variation. Try both fillings.

Eggs	3	3
Granulated sugar	¾ cup	175 mL
Cooked pumpkin (or canned, without spices)	⅔ cup	150 mL
All-purpose flour	¾ cup	175 mL
Baking powder	1 tsp.	5 mL
Cinnamon	1 tsp.	5 mL
Salt	½ tsp.	2 mL
Ginger	½ tsp.	2 mL
Nutmeg	½ tsp.	2 mL

Grease 10 x 15-inch (25 x 38 cm) jelly roll pan. Line with waxed paper. Beat eggs until frothy. Add sugar and beat until thick and light colored.

Slowly beat in pumpkin.

Sift next 6 ingredients over top. Fold in carefully. Pour into prepared pan. Bake in 375°F (190°C) oven for about 15 minutes until an inserted toothpick comes out clean. Have a tea towel with icing (confectioner's) sugar sprinkled over. Turn cake out onto sugar. Roll from short side, rolling cake and towel together. Cool. Fill with Cream Cheese Filling or Chantilly Ginger.

CREAM CHEESE FILLING

Cream cheese, softened	8 oz.	250 g
Icing (confectioner's) sugar	1 cup	250 mL
Butter or margarine	¼ cup	60 mL
Vanilla	½ tsp.	2 mL

Beat all together. Spread over cake and re-roll.

CHANTILLY GINGER

Whipping cream (or 1 env. topping)	1 cup	250 mL
Ginger snap crumbs	½ cup	125 mL

Whip cream until stiff. Fold in crumbs. Spread over cake and roll. Very tasty.

Pictured on page 17.

BOSTON CREAM PIE

It's a piece of cake!

White cake layers, 8–inch (20 cm)	2	2
FILLING		
Milk	1 cup	250 mL
All-purpose flour	¼ cup	60 mL
Granulated sugar	¼ cup	50 mL
Egg	1	1
Vanilla	½ tsp.	2 mL
GLAZE		
Icing (confectioner's) sugar	1 cup	250 mL
Cocoa	2 tbsp.	30 mL
Butter or margarine, melted	1 tbsp.	15 mL
Water or milk	4 tsp.	20 mL

Both cake layers may be used, or, if preferred, slice 1 layer to make 2 layers out of it.

Filling: Heat milk in heavy saucepan over medium heat to boiling.

Measure flour and sugar into small bowl. Stir thoroughly. Stir in egg and vanilla. Pour into milk, stirring while it boils and thickens. Cool well.

Glaze: Beat all ingredients together adding a bit more liquid if necessary to make a barely pourable glaze.

To assemble, spread custard between layers. Spread glaze over top only. If you like, allow a bit to dribble over sides. Serve with or without whipped cream. Chill at least 1 hour before serving. Serves 12.

CARROT CAKE

This is one time that you can tell a cake by its icing. Freezes well.

Granulated sugar	1 cup	250 mL
Cooking oil	1 cup	250 mL
Eggs	3	3
Vanilla	½ tsp.	2 mL
All-purpose flour	1⅓ cups	325 mL
Baking powder	1½ tsp.	8 mL
Baking soda	1½ tsp.	8 mL
Salt	½ tsp.	2 mL
Cinnamon	1½ tsp.	7 mL
Grated carrots	2 cups	500 mL

Beat sugar and cooking oil in mixing bowl. Beat in eggs, 1 at a time. Add vanilla.

Measure in next 5 ingredients. Stir to mix.

Stir in grated carrot. Turn into greased 9 x 9 inch (22 x 22 cm) pan. For a thinner cake use a 9 x 13 inch (22 x 33 cm) pan. Bake in 350°F (180°C) oven for 35 to 45 minutes until an inserted toothpick comes out clean. Cool and frost.

CREAM CHEESE ICING

Cream cheese	4 oz.	125 g
Butter or margarine	¼ cup	60 mL
Vanilla	1 tsp.	5 mL
Icing (confectioner's) sugar	2 cups	500 mL

Beat cream cheese, butter and vanilla well. Add sugar gradually, beating until fluffy. Spread over cake. May be doubled to ice a 2 layer cake or simply because of more good icing.

APPLE JACK

Tender, juicy apples covered with a cake-like topping. An old standby.

Medium apples, peeled and sliced	4	4
Granulated sugar	½ cup	125 mL
Cinnamon sprinkle		
Granulated sugar	½ cup	125 mL
Butter, margarine or drippings	2 tbsp.	30 mL
Egg	1	1
Milk	½ cup	125 mL
All-purpose flour	1¼ cups	300 mL
Baking powder	1½ tsp.	7 mL
Salt	½ tsp.	2 mL

Put apples into 8-inch (20 cm) casserole. Pour first amount of sugar evenly over top. Sprinkle with cinnamon.

Mix sugar, butter and egg together in mixing bowl. Stir in milk. Add flour, baking powder and salt. Mix well. Spoon over apples. Bake in 350°F (180°C) oven for 35 to 40 minutes until apples and cake-topping are cooked. Serve warm with ice cream or cream. Serves 6.

COTTAGE PUDDING

A cake with lots of sauce. School kids' favorite.

Granulated sugar	¾ cup	175 mL
Butter or margarine, softened	2 tbsp.	30 mL
Eggs	2	2
Vanilla	1 tsp.	5 mL
All-purpose flour	1½ cups	375 mL
Baking powder	1 tsp.	5 mL
Salt	¼ tsp.	1 mL
Milk	½ cup	125 mL

Put sugar and butter into mixing bowl. Add 1 egg and beat well. Add second egg. Beat. Stir in vanilla.

Add flour, baking powder and salt alternately with milk. Stir well. Spread in greased 9 x 9-inch (22 x 22 cm) pan. Bake in 350°F (180°C) oven for 30 minutes or until an inserted toothpick comes out clean. Cut into squares. Serve hot. Spoon Brown Sugar Sauce, page 142, over top. Serves 9 to 12.

CHOCOLATE COTTAGE PUDDING: Use Chocolate Pudding Sauce, page 142, over chocolate cake.

LEMON CHEESECAKE

A delicate lemon tone to this creamy dessert. The sour cream topping adds the finishing touch. May be frozen.

CRUST		
Butter or margarine	⅓ cup	75 mL
Vanilla wafer crumbs	1½ cups	375 mL
Brown sugar	¼ cup	50 mL
FILLING		
Cream cheese, softened	2 – 8 oz.	2 – 250 g
Eggs	3	3
Granulated sugar	1 cup	250 mL
Lemon juice	3 tbsp.	50 mL
Grated lemon rind	1 tsp.	5 mL
TOPPING		
Sour cream	2 cups	500 mL
Granulated sugar	3 tbsp.	50 mL

Crust: Melt butter in saucepan. Stir in wafer crumbs and sugar. Press into ungreased 10-inch (25 cm) springform or 9 x 9-inch (22 x 22 cm) pan. Bake in 350°F (180°C) oven for 10 minutes. Cool.

Filling: Beat cream cheese until smooth and creamy. Beat in eggs, 1 at a time. Add sugar, lemon juice and rind. Mix well. Turn into crumb-lined pan. Bake in 350°F (180°C) oven for about 45 minutes until firm.

Topping: Mix sour cream and sugar together. Spread over cheesecake. Return to oven for 10 to 12 minutes. Chill until needed. Cuts into 12 pieces.

Pictured on page 35.

A newly hatched beetle is called a baby buggy.

CHERRY CHEESECAKE

A dessert lover's glistening special.

CRUST		
Butter or margarine	½ cup	125 mL
Graham cracker crumbs	1½ cups	375 mL
FILLING		
Cream cheese, softened	8 oz.	250 g
Granulated sugar	1 cup	250 mL
Lemon juice	1 tbsp.	15 mL
Envelope of topping	1	1
Milk	½ cup	125 mL
Cherry pie filling	19 oz.	540 mL

Crust: Melt butter in saucepan over medium heat. Stir in crumbs. Press into 9 x 9–inch (22 x 22 cm) pan. Bake in 350°F (180°C) oven for 10 minutes. Cool.

Filling: Beat cheese, sugar and lemon juice together to dissolve sugar.

Whip topping with milk, as package directs, until stiff. Fold into cheese mixture and spread over base. Chill.

Spread cherry filling over top. Chill. Serves 9.

BLUEBERRY CHEESECAKE: Use blueberry pie filling instead of cherry.

Pictured on page 35.

CHEESECAKE

Delicious flavor. Lends itself towards any toppings. Creamy smooth. May be frozen.

CRUST
Butter or margarine	¼ cup	50 mL
Graham cracker crumbs	1⅓ cups	325 mL
Brown sugar	¼ cup	50 mL

FILLING
Cream cheese, softened	2 – 8 oz.	2 – 250 g
Egg yolks	5	5
Granulated sugar	1 cup	250 mL
Lemon juice	2 tbsp.	30 mL
Vanilla	1 tsp.	5 mL
Sour cream	2 cups	500 mL
Egg whites, room temperature	5	5

Crust: Melt butter in saucepan over medium heat. Stir in crumbs and sugar. Pack into ungreased 10-inch (25 cm) round springform pan or use a 9-inch (22 cm) square pan. Bake in 325°F (160°C) oven for 10 minutes.

Filling: Beat cream cheese, egg yolks, sugar, lemon juice and vanilla together well.

Mix in sour cream.

Beat egg whites until stiff. Fold into cheese mixture. Pour over crumb crust. Bake in 325°F (160°C) oven for 1 hour. Turn oven off and leave cheesecake in oven for 1 hour more. Let stand at least 2 hours. Chill until needed.

Use any fruit pie filling for topping or use a recipe under Sauces, Toppings, page 155 in Index. Cut into 12 wedges.

BEST CHOCOLATE CHEESECAKE

So rich, so smooth — the ultimate. Freezes well.

CRUST		
Butter or margarine	⅓ cup	75 mL
Graham cracker crumbs	1½ cups	350 mL
Granulated sugar	¼ cup	50 mL
Cocoa	¼ cup	50 mL
FILLING		
Cream cheese, softened	3 – 8 oz.	3 – 250 g
Granulated sugar	1 cup	250 mL
Eggs	4	4
Sour cream	1 cup	250 mL
Semisweet chocolate chips	2 cups	450 mL
Butter or margarine	½ cup	125 mL

Crust: Melt butter in saucepan. Stir in crumbs, sugar and cocoa. Mix well. Press into bottom and ¾ way up sides of ungreased 10-inch (25 cm) springform pan. Do not bake.

Filling: Beat cream cheese and sugar until blended. Add eggs, 1 at a time, beating after each addition. Mix in sour cream.

Combine chocolate chips and butter in saucepan over low heat until melted. Stir often. Add to cheese mixture. Pour into prepared pan. Bake in 325°F (160°C) oven for about 1½ hours until center is firm. Cool at room temperature, then chill. To serve, top with whipped cream and shaved chocolate.

Variation: Fold in ½ cup (125 mL) chopped pecans or walnuts before baking.

Variation: Use whipping cream in place of sour cream for a milkier chocolate flavor.

Pictured on page 35.

RASPBERRY CHEESECAKE

Creamy, luscious, no–bake masterpiece. Dieter's dilemma!

CRUST		
Butter or margarine	½ cup	125 mL
Graham cracker crumbs	2 cups	500 mL
Brown sugar, packed	¼ cup	50 mL
FILLING		
Raspberry flavored gelatin	2 - 3 oz.	2-85 g
Boiling water	1 cup	250 mL
Frozen raspberries, partly thawed	15 oz.	425 g
Cream cheese, softened	2 – 8 oz.	2 – 250 g
Icing (confectioner's) sugar	¾ cup	175 mL
Envelopes of topping	2	2
Milk	1 cup	225 mL

Crust: Melt butter in saucepan. Stir in crumbs and sugar. Pack into ungreased 9 x 13–inch (22 x 23 cm) pan. Bake in 350°F (180°C) oven for 10 minutes or use without baking.

Filling: Dissolve gelatin in water. Stir in berries. Chill until syrupy.

Beat cream cheese and icing sugar together until blended.

Prepare topping with milk as directed on the package. Fold into cheese mixture. Fold into thickened jelly. Pour over crust. Chill. Makes 15 servings.

Pictured on page 35.

Women who play with fire prefer men with money to burn.

PUMPKIN CHEESECAKE

A pretty contrast — pumpkin color on a dark ginger snap crust. As good as it looks. Make a day ahead. Freezes well.

CRUST		
Butter or margarine	¼ cup	50 mL
Ginger snaps, crushed	1¼ cups	300 mL
FILLING		
Cream cheese, softened	2 – 8 oz.	2 – 250 g
Granulated sugar	⅔ cup	150 mL
Eggs	2	2
Canned pumpkin (without spices)	14 oz.	398 mL
Cinnamon	½ tsp.	3 mL
Nutmeg	½ tsp.	2 mL
Ginger	½ tsp.	2 mL
Salt	½ tsp.	2 mL

Crust: Melt butter in saucepan. Stir in crumbs. Press into ungreased 9 × 9–inch (22 × 22 cm) pan. Bake in 350°F (180°C) oven for 10 minutes.

Filling: Beat cream cheese and sugar together well. Add eggs, 1 at a time, beating after each addition. Mix in remaining ingredients. Pour over crust. Bake in 350°F (180°C) oven for about 50 to 60 minutes or until firm. Chill. Garnish with whipped cream and chocolate curls. Serves 12.

Pictured on page 35.

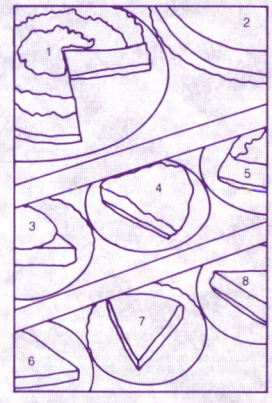

1. Pumpkin Cheesecake page 34.
2. Raspberry Cheesecake page 33.
3. Best Chocolate Cheesecake page 32.
4. Cherry Cheesecake page 30.
5. Lemon Chiffon Cheesecake page 37.
6. Lemon Cheesecake page 29.
7. Praline Cheesecake page 39.
8. Chocolate Swirl Cheesecake page 38.

LEMON CHIFFON CHEESECAKE

A frothy delicate delight both to the eye and the palate. A no-bake wonder.

CRUST		
Butter or margarine	¼ cup	50 mL
Graham cracker crumbs	1¼ cups	300 mL
Granulated sugar	2 tbsp.	30 mL
FILLING		
Unflavored gelatin	2 – ¼ oz.	2 – 7 g
Cold water	½ cup	125 mL
Egg yolks	2	2
Milk	½ cup	125 mL
Granulated sugar	1 cup	250 mL
Salt	1 tsp.	5 mL
Creamed cottage cheese, blender smoothed (or sieved)	2 cups	500 mL
Grated rind and juice of lemon	1	1
Lemon juice	2 tbsp.	30 mL
Vanilla	1 tsp.	5 mL
Egg whites	2	2
Whipping cream (or 1 env. topping)	1 cup	250 mL

Crust: Melt butter in saucepan. Add crumbs and sugar. Stir to mix. Pack into bottom and sides of ungreased 9-inch (22 cm) springform or 8 x 8-inch (20 x 20 cm) pan. Chill.

Filling: Sprinkle gelatin over water in top of double boiler. Let stand 5 minutes. Place over boiling water.

Add yolks and beat with spoon. Stir in milk, sugar and salt. Heat and stir over hot water until gelatin and sugar are dissolved. Chill until syrupy.

Fold cottage cheese, rind, lemon juice and vanilla into thickening gelatin.

Whip egg whites until stiff, then using same beater, beat cream until stiff. Fold in egg whites, then fold in whipped cream. Pour over crumbs. Chill. Serve with or without Lemon Sauce, page 141. Garnish with lemon slice. Serves 12.

Pictured on page 35.

CHOCOLATE SWIRL CHEESECAKE

A real beauty, smooth and creamy. Best made a day ahead. May be frozen.

CRUST
Butter or margarine	⅓ cup	75 mL
Graham cracker crumbs	1½ cups	350 mL
Granulated sugar	2 tbsp.	30 mL
Cocoa	2 tbsp.	30 mL

FILLING
Cream cheese, softened	3 – 8 oz.	3 – 250 g
Granulated sugar	1 cup	250 mL
All–purpose flour	3 tbsp.	50 mL
Eggs	5	5
Vanilla	1½ tsp.	7 mL
Sour cream	1 cup	250 mL
Reserved cheese mixture	1½ cups	350 mL
Unsweetened chocolate squares, melted	2	2

Crust: Melt butter in saucepan. Stir in crumbs, sugar and cocoa. Press into bottom of ungreased 9–inch (22 cm) springform or 9 × 9 inch (22 × 22 cm) pan. Bake in 350°F (180°C) oven for 10 minutes.

Filling: Beat cream cheese, sugar and flour in mixing bowl until blended.

Beat in eggs, 1 at a time, until mixed. Add vanilla and sour cream. Mix. Measure out 1½ cups (375 mL) and reserve. Pour remaining mixture over crumbs.

Mix reserved cheese mixture with melted chocolate. Drizzle over top of cheese mixture in pan. Cut through batter in a zig–zag motion to get a swirl effect. Bake in 350°F (180°C) oven for about 1 hour or until set. Serves 12.

Pictured on page 35.

PRALINE CHEESECAKE

Mouth watering, a delicious praline flavor. Best made a day ahead. May be frozen.

CRUST		
Butter or margarine	¼ cup	50 mL
Graham cracker crumbs	1 cup	250 mL
Brown sugar, packed	2 tbsp.	30 mL
FILLING		
Cream cheese, softened	3 – 8 oz.	3 – 250 g
Brown sugar, packed (dark is best)	1¼ cups	300 g
All–purpose flour	2 tbsp.	30 mL
Eggs	4	4
Vanilla	1½ tsp.	7 mL
Chopped pecans	½ cup	125 mL
TOPPING		
Maple syrup or maple flavored pancake syrup	1 tbsp.	15 mL

Crust: Melt butter in saucepan. Stir in crumbs and sugar. Pack into bottom of ungreased 9–inch (22 cm) springform or 8 × 8–inch (20 × 20 cm) pan. Bake in 350°F (180°C) oven for 10 minutes.

Filling: Beat cheese, sugar and flour together at medium speed until blended.

Add eggs, 1 at a time, beating until blended after each addition. Mix in vanilla and nuts. Pour over crust. Bake in 350°F (180°C) oven for 50 to 60 minutes until firm. Chill.

Topping: Spread syrup over top of cooled cheesecake. Chill. Serves 12.

MAPLE WALNUT CHEESECAKE: Omit vanilla and pecans. Add 1½ tsp. (7 mL) maple flavoring and ½–1 cup (125–250 mL) chopped walnuts.

CREAMY PRALINE CHEESECAKE: Add 1 cup (250 mL) sour cream after the eggs. Gives a creamier texture.

Pictured on page 35.

PUMPKIN CREAM SQUARES

A great refrigerator dessert requiring no baking.

CRUST		
Butter or margarine	1/3 cup	75 mL
Graham cracker crumbs	1 1/2 cups	375 mL
Granulated sugar	1/4 cup	50 mL
FILLING		
Unflavored gelatin powder	1/4 oz.	7 g
Cold water	3/4 cup	175 mL
Granulated sugar	1/2 cup	125 mL
Salt	1/2 tsp.	2 mL
Cinnamon	1/2 tsp.	2 mL
Nutmeg	1/2 tsp.	2 mL
Ginger	1/2 tsp.	2 mL
Canned pumpkin (without spices)	14 oz.	398 mL
Whipping cream	1 cup	250 mL

Crust: Melt butter in saucepan. Stir in crumbs and sugar. Press into ungreased 9 x 9–inch (22 x 22 cm) pan. Bake in 350°F (180°C) oven for 10 minutes.

Filling: Sprinkle gelatin over water in saucepan. Let stand 5 minutes. Heat, stirring, over medium heat to dissolve.

Mix sugar, salt, cinnamon, nutmeg and ginger together well. Stir into gelatin. Remove from heat. Add pumpkin and mix. Chill until it shows signs of thickening.

Whip cream until stiff. Fold into thickened mixture. Spread over crumb crust. Serve with a dollop of whipped cream to 9 thankful guests.

DANISH CREAM SQUARES

This creamy dessert will certainly spark conversation. Delightful to look at. Delightful to eat.

Graham crackers		
Vanilla pudding and pie filling, 6 serving size	1	1
Milk	2½ cups	575 mL
Whipping cream (or 1 env. topping)	1 cup	250 mL
Granulated sugar	1 tbsp.	15 mL
Vanilla	½ tsp.	2 mL
Graham crackers		
Icing (confectioner's) sugar	1½ cups	350 mL
Milk	3 tbsp.	50 mL
Square of semisweet chocolate	1	1
Butter or margarine	1 tsp.	5 mL

Line 9 x 13-inch (22 x 33 cm) ungreased pan with whole graham crackers, trimming to fit.

Cook pudding with milk as directed on package using 2½ cups (575 mL) milk. Allow to cool. Spread over crackers in pan.

Beat cream, sugar and vanilla until stiff. Spread over pudding.

Put on another layer of whole graham crackers, trimming to fit.

Mix icing sugar and milk together well. Add more sugar or milk if needed to make a fairly runny glaze. Spread over cracker layer.

Melt chocolate with butter over hot water. Drizzle over top. Chill. Let stand overnight before using. Cuts into 15 pieces.

PINK LADY

Lots of flavors here. Raspberry, pineapple and strawberry combine to make this a winning dessert.

CRUST
Butter or margarine	½ cup	125 mL
Graham cracker crumbs	2 cups	500 mL
Granulated sugar	⅓ cup	75 mL

FILLING
Juice from pineapple plus water	1 cup	225 mL
Large marshmallows	16	16
Raspberry flavored gelatin	3 oz.	85 g
Boiling water	1 cup	250 mL
Cold water	1 cup	200 mL
Sliced fresh strawberries	1 cup	250 mL
Pineapple chunks, diced	14 oz.	398 mL
Whipping cream (or 1 env. topping)	1 cup	250 mL
Slivered almonds	½ cup	125 mL
Vanilla	½ tsp.	2 mL

Coconut

Crust: Melt butter in saucepan. Stir in crumbs and sugar. Press ⅔ into ungreased 8 × 8–inch (20 × 20 cm) pan.

Filling: Put juice and marshmallows into top of double boiler. Heat over simmering water, stirring often, until melted.

Dissolve gelatin in boiling water. Add cold water. Stir into marshmallow mixture. Chill until syrupy.

Add strawberries and pineapple.

Whip cream until stiff. Fold in nuts and vanilla. Fold into thickened mixture. Pour ½ mixture over prepared crust. Sprinkle with remaining crumbs. Spoon second ½ cream mixture over top.

Sprinkle with coconut. Chill. Serves 9.

LAYERED LEMON

So refreshing. Absolutely luscious. A favorite refrigerator dessert.

FIRST LAYER
All-purpose flour	2 cups	500 mL
Butter or margarine	1 cup	250 mL
Finely chopped pecans	1 cup	250 mL

SECOND LAYER
Cream cheese, softened	2 – 8 oz.	2 – 250 g
Icing (confectioner's) sugar	1 cup	250 mL
Whipping cream (or 1 env. topping)	1 cup	250 mL

THIRD LAYER
Lemon pie fillings (not instant) enough for 2 pies	2	2

FOURTH LAYER
Whipping cream (or 2 env. topping)	2 cups	500 mL
Granulated sugar	2 tbsp.	30 mL
Vanilla	1 tsp.	5 mL

First Layer: Mix flour, butter and nuts together until crumbly. Press into 9 × 13–inch (22 × 33 cm) pan. Bake in 350°F (180°C) oven for 15 minutes. Cool.

Second Layer: Beat cheese and icing sugar together well. Beat whipping cream until stiff. Fold into cream cheese mixture. Spread over cooled crust.

Third Layer: Prepare lemon pie fillings according to directions on package. Cool, stirring often. Pour over cheese layer.

Fourth layer: Beat cream, sugar and vanilla until stiff. Spread over lemon layer. Garnish with chopped pecans or slivered almonds. Makes 15 generous pieces.

Pictured on page 53.

INSTANT LEMON DESSERT

A quick trick, mellow and smooth.

CRUST		
Butter or margarine	¼ cup	50 mL
Graham cracker crumbs	1¼ cups	300 mL
Brown sugar, packed	¼ cup	50 mL
FILLING		
Cream cheese, softened	4 oz.	125 g
Instant lemon pudding, 4 serving size	1	1
Milk	1½ cups	350 mL

Crust: Melt butter in saucepan. Stir in crumbs and sugar. Measure ⅓ cup (75 mL) crumbs and reserve. Press remaining crumbs into ungreased 8 × 8–inch (20 × 20 cm) pan.

Filling: Cut cream cheese into blender. Use beater if you don't have a blender. Add pudding powder and milk. Blend until smooth. Pour over crumb base. Top with reserved crumbs. Chill several hours. Serves 6.

STRAWBERRY BAVARIAN

A quick dessert for a hot summer day or anytime.

Strawberry flavored gelatin	3 oz.	85 g
Boiling water	1 cup	250 mL
Frozen sliced strawberries with juice, partly thawed	15 oz.	425 g
Whipping cream (or 1 env. topping)	1 cup	250 mL

Dissolve gelatin in boiling water.

Add strawberries. Stir until mixed. Chill until syrupy.

Beat cream until stiff. Fold into thickened mixture. Pour into pretty bowl or over 9 × 9–inch (22 × 22 cm) crumb crust in pan. See crust recipe above. Looks especially attractive on a chocolate crumb crust. See page 78 or 79. Chill. Serves 9.

CHERRY BANANA SLICE

A pretty fruited bavarian-type dessert. Luscious!

CRUST		
Butter or margarine	½ cup	125 mL
Vanilla wafer crumbs	1½ cups	350 mL
FILLING		
Raspberry flavored gelatin	3 oz.	85 g
Boiling water	1 cup	225 mL
Cherry pie filling	19 oz.	540 mL
Cream cheese, softened	4 oz.	125 g
Granulated sugar	⅓ cup	75 mL
Whipping cream (or 1 env. topping)	1 cup	250 mL
Tiny marshmallows	1 cup	250 mL
Small bananas, sliced	2	2

Crust: Melt butter in saucepan. Stir in crumbs. Reserve ½ cup (125 mL). Press remaining crumbs into ungreased 9 × 9-inch (22 × 22 cm) pan.

Filling: Dissolve gelatin in boiling water. Stir in pie filling. Chill until syrupy.

Beat cream cheese and sugar until fluffy. Set aside.

Beat cream until stiff. Fold in marshmallows, bananas and cheese mixture. Fold into thickened gelatin. Turn into prepared crust. Scatter reserved crumbs over top. Chill. Serves 9.

Nowadays a hot school lunch isn't a warm meal. It's a stolen sandwich.

BANANA SPLIT DESSERT

One that won't melt! So good, so light.

CRUST		
Butter or margarine	½ cup	125 mL
Graham cracker crumbs	2 cups	500 mL
Brown sugar	¼ cup	50 mL
FILLING		
Crushed pineapple, drained	19 oz.	540 mL
Icing (confectioner's) sugar	4 cups	1 L
Eggs (see Note)	2	2
Butter or margarine, softened	1 cup	250 mL
Vanilla	2 tsp.	10 mL
Medium oranges, optional	2	2
Large bananas	3	3
Whipping cream (or 2 env. topping)	2 cups	500 mL
Graham cracker crumbs, chopped nuts and cherries		

Crust: Melt butter in medium saucepan over medium heat. Stir in crumbs and sugar. Press in ungreased 9 x 13-inch (22 x 33 cm) pan. Use as is or bake in 350°F (180°C) oven for 10 minutes. Cool.

Filling: Scatter pineapple evenly over base.

Put sugar, eggs, butter and vanilla into mixing bowl. Beat for about 10 minutes. Spread over pineapple.

Peel oranges. Cut into thin slices, then cut each slice into 2 or 3 pieces. Layer over filling. Layer thin slices of banana over top.

Whip cream until stiff. Spread over fruit. Sprinkle with a mixture of crumbs, nuts and cherries or only use 1 item for topping if preferred, or spoon on chocolate sauce or leave plain. Cuts into 18 pieces.

Note: If you prefer not to use raw eggs, add 2 tbsp. (30 mL) milk instead. Mixture will not beat up as smoothly and will be a bit softer.

LEMON SNOW

Light and delicate with a good lemon flavor. White with tiny bits of lemon showing through.

Unflavored gelatin powder	¼ oz.	7 g
Cold water	¼ cup	50 mL
Hot water	1 cup	250 mL
Granulated sugar	¾ cup	175 mL
Grated lemon rind	1 tsp.	5 mL
Lemon juice	¼ cup	50 mL
Salt	¼ tsp.	1 mL
Egg whites	2	2

Sprinkle gelatin over cold water in small saucepan. Let stand for 5 minutes.

Add hot water and sugar. Stir over medium heat until sugar is dissolved.

Stir in lemon rind, juice and salt. Chill until syrupy, then beat until frothy.

Beat egg whites until stiff. Fold into gelatin mixture. Turn into mold or serving bowl. Chill.

Save time. Water your garden with beer and get stewed vegetables.

LEMON JELLY DESSERT

A light dessert, sort of like a cheesecake without any cheese. Slight lemon flavor. Just right after a heavy meal.

CRUST
Graham cracker crumbs, good sprinkle

FILLING
Lemon flavored gelatin	3 oz.	85 g
Boiling water	1 cup	250 mL
Cold water	½ cup	100 mL
Evaporated milk, freezer chilled	14 oz.	385 mL
Granulated sugar	1 cup	250 mL
Juice of lemon	1	1

Graham cracker crumbs, good sprinkle

Crust: Sprinkle crumbs, to cover, over bottom of ungreased 9 × 9–inch (22 × 22 cm) pan or if you would like more not–so–deep servings use 9 × 13–inch (22 × 33 cm) pan.

Filling: Stir gelatin with boiling water to dissolve. Add cold water. Chill until syrupy.

Beat partially frozen milk until soft peaks form. Add sugar and lemon juice. Beat again until quite stiff. Beat in thickened jelly. Carefully pour filling over crumbs. Smooth top.

Sprinkle crumbs over top. Chill. Serves 9 generously.

An illegally parked frog gets toad away.

CHOCOLATE PINEAPPLE DESSERT

The hint of pineapple is complemented by the chocolate crust. Refreshing.

CRUST		
Butter or margarine	½ cup	125 mL
Graham cracker crumbs	2 cups	500 mL
Granulated sugar	¼ cup	50 mL
Cocoa	¼ cup	50 mL
FILLING		
Unflavored gelatin powder	¼ oz.	7 g
Cold water	⅓ cup	75 mL
Boiling water	⅓ cup	75 mL
Juice of lemon	1	1
Salt	⅛ tsp.	0.5 mL
Egg whites beaten stiff (optional — gives more volume)	3	3
Granulated sugar	½ cup	125 mL
Vanilla	½ tsp.	2 mL
Crushed pineapple, drained well	14 oz.	398 mL
Whipping cream (or 1 env. topping)	1 cup	250 mL

Crust: Melt butter in medium saucepan over medium heat. Stir in crumbs, sugar and cocoa. Measure ½ cup (125 mL) for topping. Press remaining crumbs into ungreased 9 x 13–inch (22 x 33 cm) pan.

Filling: Sprinkle gelatin over cold water in small saucepan. Let stand for 5 minutes.

Add boiling water, lemon juice and salt. Heat, stirring, over medium heat until dissolved. Chill until syrupy.

Fold in egg whites, (if using), sugar, vanilla and pineapple.

Whip cream until stiff. Fold in. Pour over chocolate crust. Smooth top. Scatter reserved crumbs over all. Chill. Cuts into 12 or 15 pieces.

BLACK FOREST SOUFFLÉ

Light as a chocolate feather.

Canned cherries, dark or sour, drained and pitted	14 oz.	398 mL
Unflavored gelatin powders	2 – ¼ oz.	2 – 7 g
Granulated sugar	½ cup	125 mL
Egg yolks	3	3
Milk	2 cups	500 mL
Semisweet chocolate chips	⅔ cup	150 mL
Vanilla	1½ tsp.	7 mL
Brandy flavoring	½ tsp.	2 mL
Egg whites	3	3
Whipping cream (or 2 env. topping)	2 cups	500 mL

Set a few cherries aside to be used as a garnish. Cut remaining cherries into quarters.

Stir gelatin and sugar together in medium saucepan. Mix in egg yolks and milk. Heat over low heat until gelatin is dissolved and eggs are cooked, about 5 minutes.

Add chocolate chips, vanilla and brandy flavoring. Stir to melt chips. Chill until syrupy, stirring occasionally.

Beat egg whites until stiff. Using same beaters, beat cream until stiff. Fold egg whites into gelatin mixture, then fold in cream. Fold in cut up cherries. Pour into 4–cup (1 L) soufflé dish with 3 inch (8 cm) collar fastened around it. Chill. Garnish with cherries and shaved or grated chocolate. Cover side edge with crushed nuts if desired.

ZUCCOTTO

Such an elegant dessert. A chocolate cake mold filled with a combination of chocolate, cherries and cream. Easier to make than it looks.

Chocolate cake layer, 9 inch (22 cm)	1	1
Orange juice	¼ cup	50 mL
Brandy flavoring	¼ tsp.	1 mL
Whipping cream (or 1 env. topping)	1 cup	250 mL
Icing (confectioner's) sugar	2 tbsp.	30 mL
Toasted hazelnuts	¼ cup	50 mL
Canned cherries, drained, halved and pitted (or fresh)	½ cup	125 mL
Semisweet chocolate squares, grated	2	2

Cut cake layer into 2 layers. Choose an 8-cup (2 L) gently rounded bowl. Ease 1 layer inside of bowl, pushing down to form a shell. If it breaks, fit in as best you can. Mix orange juice and flavoring together. Sprinkle over shell.

Whip cream and sugar together until stiff.

Fold in nuts, cherries and chocolate. Spoon into cake shell. If top of mold is smaller than second cake layer (it should be about 7¼ inches, 18 cm) trim to fit. Place over cream mixture. Chill at least 4 hours. Unmold onto serving plate. Slice into 6 or 8 wedges for some very lucky people.

Pictured on page 53.

When the robot ran down, it stated simply "AC come, AC go".

MAPLE BAVARIAN

A smooth dessert, this is one of the best ways to use maple syrup.

Unflavored gelatin	¼ oz.	7 g
Water	½ cup	125 mL
Maple Syrup	1 cup	250 mL
Eggs	3	3
Salt	¼ tsp.	1 mL
Milk	½ cup	125 mL
Whipping cream (or 1 env. topping)	1 cup	250 mL

Sprinkle gelatin over water in top of double boiler. Let stand 5 minutes. Place over simmering water. Stir to dissolve.

Add maple syrup. Mix in eggs thoroughly, 1 at a time. Stir in salt and milk. Cook and stir until mixture coats metal spoon. Remove from heat. Chill until it begins to thicken. Stir occasionally.

Whip cream until stiff. Fold into egg mixture. Pour into mold or pretty bowl. Served with extra whipped cream if desired.

1. Zuccotto page 51.
2. Layered Lemon page 43.
3. Raspberry–Mallow Squares page 56.

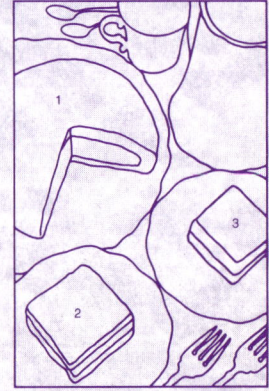

PINEAPPLE DELIGHT

Although this is an extra-special favorite, be sure to try the strawberry variation. So showy. So good.

CRUST		
Butter or margarine	½ cup	125 mL
Graham cracker crumbs	2 cups	500 mL
Granulated sugar	¼ cup	50 mL
FILLING		
Icing (confectioner's) sugar	1½ cups	375 mL
Butter or margarine, softened	½ cup	125 mL
Eggs (See Note)	2	2
Crushed pineapple, drained	19 oz.	540 mL
Whipping cream (or 1 env. topping)	1 cup	250 mL

Crust: Melt butter in saucepan over medium heat. Stir in crumbs and sugar. Reserve 1 cup (250 mL) for topping. Press remaining crumbs into ungreased 9 × 13-inch (22 × 33 cm) pan. Bake in 350°F (180°C) oven for 10 minutes. Cool.

Filling: Beat icing sugar and butter together well. Add eggs, 1 at a time, beating until smooth. Spread over crumb layer.

Scatter pineapple over top. Whip cream until stiff. Spread over pineapple. Pineapple may be folded into cream, if desired, before spreading. Sprinkle with reserved crumbs. Cuts into 15 pieces.

Note: If you prefer not to use raw eggs, add 2 tbsp. (30 mL) milk instead. Mixture will not beat up as smoothly and will be a bit softer.

STRAWBERRY DELIGHT: Omit pineapple. Drain juice from 15 oz. (425 g) frozen sliced strawberries. Stir in 1 tbsp. (15 mL) cornstarch. Heat and stir until boiling and thickened. Cool. Stir in berries and use in place of pineapple. Makes a pretty red layer and is delicious.

RASPBERRY-MALLOW SQUARES

A gorgeous red ribbon between a white shortbread base and a melted marshmallow top.

CRUST		
All-purpose flour	1 cup	250 mL
Butter or margarine	½ cup	125 mL
Granulated sugar	2 tbsp.	30 mL
FILLING		
Raspberry flavored gelatin	3 oz.	85 g
Boiling water	1 cup	225 mL
Frozen raspberries, partly thawed	15 oz.	425 g
Large white marshmallows	32	32
Milk	½ cup	125 mL
Whipping cream (or 1 env. topping)	1 cup	250 mL

Crust: Mix flour, butter and sugar until crumbly. Press into ungreased 9 x 9-inch (22 x 22 cm) pan. Bake in 325°F (160°C) oven for 15 minutes.

Filling: Stir gelatin and water together until dissolved. Add raspberries. Mix together. Chill until syrupy. Pour over crumbs. Chill.

Melt marshmallows in milk in top of double boiler. Cool.

Whip cream until stiff. Fold into cooled marshmallow mixture. Spread over firm raspberry jelly. Chill. Cuts into 9 servings.

Pictured on page 53.

You will be sure to get your name in the paper if you walk across the street reading one.

SIX LAYER DESSERT

This is a creamy dish that somewhere along the line became known as Sex In A Pan. No doubt it was miscopied from Six In a Pan.

CRUST
Butter or margarine	½ cup	125 mL
All-purpose flour	1 cup	250 mL
Granulated sugar	2 tbsp.	30 mL
Finely chopped nuts (optional)	½ cup	125 mL

FILLING
Cream cheese, softened	8 oz.	250 g
Icing (confectioner's) sugar	1 cup	250 mL
Whipping cream (or 1 env. topping)	1 cup	250 mL
Instant Chocolate Pudding, 4 serving size	1	1
Milk	1½ cups	350 mL
Instant Vanilla Pudding, 4 serving size	1	1
Milk	1½ cups	350 mL

Crust: Melt butter in saucepan. Stir in flour, sugar and nuts. Press in a 9 x 13-inch (22 x 33 cm) pan. Bake in 325°F (160°C) oven for about 15 minutes. Cool.

Filling: Blend cream cheese and icing sugar together well. Spread over cooled base.

Whip cream until stiff. Spread ½ over cheese layer.

Beat chocolate pudding mix with first amount of milk for 2 minutes. Pour over cream layer.

Beat vanilla pudding mix with second amount of milk for 2 minutes. Pour over chocolate layer.

Top with second ½ whipped cream. May be garnished with shaved chocolate. Chill overnight. Makes 12 pieces.

BROKEN GLASS

Although this appears to be lengthy, it really isn't difficult to make. Very colorful.

CRUST		
Butter or margarine	½ cup	125 mL
Graham cracker crumbs	2 cups	500 mL
Brown sugar, packed	¼ cup	50 mL

FILLING		
Raspberry flavored gelatin	3 oz.	85 g
Boiling water	1½ cups	350 mL
Lime flavored gelatin	3 oz.	85 g
Boiling water	1½ cups	350 mL
Lemon flavored gelatin	3 oz.	85 g
Boiling water	1½ cups	350 mL
Unflavored gelatin powder	¼ oz.	7 g
Cold water	¼ cup	50 mL
Pineapple juice	1 cup	250 mL
Whipping cream (or 2 env. topping)	2 cups	500 mL
Granulated sugar	2 tbsp.	30 mL
Vanilla	1 tsp.	5 mL

Crust: Melt butter in saucepan. Stir in crumbs and sugar. Press into ungreased 9 x 13–inch (22 x 33 cm) pan. Bake in 350°F (180°C) oven for 10 minutes.

Filling: Dissolve raspberry gelatin in first amount of water. Pour into pan so it will be about ¼ inch (¾ cm) thick. Chill.

Dissolve lime gelatin in second amount of water. Pour into pan so it will be about ¼ inch (¾ cm) thick. Chill.

Dissolve lemon gelatin in third amount of water. Pour into pan so it will be about ¼ inch (¾ cm) thick. Chill.

Sprinkle unflavored gelatin over cold water in small saucepan. Let stand 5 minutes. Add pineapple juice. Heat and stir over medium heat until dissolved. Chill until syrupy.

Whip cream, sugar and vanilla until stiff. Fold into thickened pineapple mixture. Draw knife through red, green and yellow jellies, cutting into ¼ inch (¾ cm) cubes. Fold cubes into cream mixture. Spoon over crumb crust. Chill. Cuts into 15 pieces.

MARSHMALLOW FRUIT SQUARES

Although this can be made any time of year by using canned peaches, fresh or frozen give more of a flavor boost.

CRUST
Butter or margarine	¼ cup	50 mL
Graham cracker crumbs	1¼ cups	300 mL
Granulated sugar	2 tbsp.	30 mL

FILLING
Large marshmallows	32	32
Milk	½ cup	125 mL
Whipping cream (or 1 env. topping)	1 cup	250 mL
Fresh medium peaches (or strawberries)	5	5

Crust: Melt butter in saucepan. Stir in crumbs and sugar. Reserve ½ cup (125 mL) for topping. Press remainder in ungreased 9 x 9–inch (22 x 22 cm) pan.

Filling: Put marshmallows and milk in top of double boiler over simmering water. Melt, stirring often. Remove from heat. Cool.

Beat cream until stiff. Fold into cooled marshmallow mixture. Fold in sliced fruit. Pour over graham base. Sprinkle reserved crumbs over top. Chill. Serves 9 generously.

MARSHMALLOW CHIP SQUARES: Omit fruit. Add 1 cup (250 mL) semisweet chocolate chips, or more if you want.

Variation: To make this any season, use 2 – 14 oz. (398 mL) cans of peaches, drained and sliced.

Priests get their travelling expenses from mass transportation.

DANISH SOUFFLÉ

Cool and creamy, you will find this pure ecstasy.

Egg yolks	4	4
Granulated sugar	½ cup	125 mL
Dark rum (or use water with 1½ tsp., 7 mL, rum flavoring)	¼ cup	50 mL
Unflavored gelatin powder	¼ oz.	7 g
Water	¼ cup	50 mL
Egg whites	4	4
Granulated sugar	½ cup	125 mL
Whipping cream (or 1 env. topping)	1 cup	250 mL
Whipped cream, chocolate curls, cherries for garnish		

Beat egg yolks, first amount of sugar and rum in mixing bowl until light colored and thickened.

Sprinkle gelatin over water in small saucepan. Let stand 5 minutes, then heat to dissolve. Add egg yolk mixture. Stir and heat just until it begins to boil. Remove from heat. Cool in large bowl.

Beat egg whites until soft peaks form. Gradually beat in second amount of sugar until stiff.

With same beaters, beat cream until stiff. Fold egg whites into egg yolk mixture. Fold in cream. Turn into pretty glass bowl or soufflé dish with collar.

Garnish with additional whipped cream, chocolate curls and cherries. Serves 10.

Their telephone bill proves that talk isn't cheap.

MINT DESSERT

A cool, minty, melt-in-your-mouth finale. Leave it white or tint pale green or pink. Showy with chocolate crumb base.

CRUST		
Butter or margarine	½ cup	125 mL
Graham cracker crumbs	2 cups	500 mL
Granulated sugar	¼ cup	50 mL
Cocoa	¼ cup	50 mL
FILLING		
Milk	1 cup	250 mL
Package of white marshmallows	8 oz.	250 g
Whipping cream (or 2 env. topping)	2 cups	500 mL
Crème De Menthe, green	½ cup	125 mL

Crust: Melt butter in saucepan. Stir in crumbs, sugar and cocoa. Press ⅔ crumb mixture into ungreased 9 x 13-inch (22 x 33 cm) pan. No need to bake.

Filling: Put milk and marshmallows in large saucepan over low heat to melt. Stir often. Allow to cool.

Whip cream until stiff. Add crème de menthe. Fold into cooled marshmallow mixture. Pour over crumb crust. Scatter remaining crumbs over top. The top may be left plain also. Chill. Cuts into 15 pieces.

Note: To tint pink, use clear crème de menthe and red food coloring. Peppermint flavoring to taste, ¼ – ½ tsp. (1 – 2 mL) may be substituted.

One thing about telephone wires being so high is that it keeps up the conversation.

CHOCOLATE MOUSSE

There are times when one craves a good chocolate mousse.

Semisweet chocolate chips	1 cup	250 mL
Water	¼ cup	60 mL
Instant coffee granules, crushed to a powder	½ tsp.	2 mL
Egg yolks	4	4
Egg whites	4	4
Granulated sugar	¼ cup	50 mL

Melt chocolate chips and water over hot (not boiling) water. Stir in coffee granules.

Beat egg yolks until light colored. Add to chocolate mixture beating to ensure there are no lumps. Remove from heat. Cool.

Beat egg whites until stiff. Gradually beat in sugar until stiff. Fold into chocolate mixture. Pour into sherbets or fruit nappies. Chill several hours. May be made a day ahead. Serve with a dab of whipped cream garnished with grated chocolate. Makes 6 servings.

GLORIFIED RICE

Dress up leftover rice with colored marshmallows, pineapple and whipped cream.

Cooked rice	1½ cups	375 mL
Crushed pineapple, drained	14 oz.	398 mL
Small marshmallows	1 cup	250 mL
Whipping cream (or 1 env. topping)	1 cup	250 mL
Granulated sugar	3 tbsp.	50 mL
Vanilla	1 tsp.	5 mL
Maraschino cherries or slivered almonds, toasted		

Combine rice, pineapple and marshmallows in bowl.

Beat cream, sugar and vanilla until stiff. Fold into rice mixture. Garnish with cherries or nuts. Chill at least 2 hours. Serves 6.

Variation: Add ¼ cup (50 mL) each of chopped maraschino cherries and chopped nuts.

Variation: Omit pineapple. Add 14 oz. (398 mL) can of fruit cocktail, drained.

COFFEE CARAMEL

A light dessert fit for any company. Almonds give an added touch. A convenient make-ahead.

Water	1 cup	250 mL
Unflavored gelatin powder	¼ oz.	7 g
Granulated sugar	¼ cup	50 mL
Slivered almonds	¼ cup	50 mL
Instant coffee granules	1 tsp.	5 mL
Whipping cream (or ½ env. topping)	½ cup	125 mL

Measure water in cup. Sprinkle gelatin over top. Let stand for 5 minutes.

Put sugar in heavy saucepan over medium heat. Melt, stirring, until a rich golden-brown. Add water-gelatin mixture, stirring well to dissolve. It will sputter at first but will settle down and dissolve as you stir.

Add almonds and coffee. Remove from heat. Chill until syrupy, stirring occasionally.

Whip cream until stiff. Fold into sugar-gelatin mixture. Turn into pretty bowl. Chill. Serves 6.

QUICK JELLIED DESSERT

Serve this yummy dessert the same day it is prepared for maximum volume.

Raspberry flavored gelatin, 4 serving size	1	1
Boiling water	1 cup	250 mL
Cold water	1 cup	200 mL
Vanilla ice cream	2 cups	500 mL

Combine gelatin and boiling water in mixing bowl. Stir to dissolve. Add cold water. Chill until firm.

Beat firm jelly well. Add ice cream and beat until well blended. Pour into serving bowl. Chill. Spoon into sherbets or fruit nappies. Serves 8.

RASPBERRY SWIRL

This is as picturesque in a pretty bowl with pink and white swirls as it is on a crust. Strawberries make a good variation.

CRUST		
Butter or margarine	½ cup	125 mL
All-purpose flour	1 cup	250 mL
Granulated sugar	2 tbsp.	30 mL
FILLING		
Raspberry flavored gelatin	3 oz.	85 g
Boiling water	¾ cup	175 mL
Frozen raspberries, partly thawed	½ of 15 oz.	½ of 425 g
Milk	½ cup	125 mL
Large marshmallows	16	16
Whipping cream (or 1 env. topping)	1 cup	250 mL

Crust: Crumble butter, flour and sugar until mealy. Press into ungreased 9 x 9-inch (22 x 22 cm) pan. Bake in 350°F (180°C) oven for about 15 minutes or until golden. Cool.

Filling: Dissolve gelatin in water. Stir in berries. Chill until syrupy.

Combine milk and marshmallows in top of double boiler. Heat over boiling water, stirring occasionally until melted. Cool.

Whip cream until stiff. Fold marshmallow mixture into cream. Fold into raspberry mixture, stopping while it is still streaky. Pour into prepared pan. Chill. Serves 9.

If you get hit on the head, your insurance company most likely will settle for a lump sum.

PEACHES AND CREAM

Fluffy and creamy. The cream cheese in the topping gives a distinctive flavor.

CRUST
Butter or margarine	½ cup	125 mL
Graham cracker crumbs	2 cups	500 mL
Brown sugar	⅓ cup	75 mL

FILLING
Sliced peaches, drained, reserve juice	2 – 14 oz.	2 – 398 mL
Reserved juice plus water to make	2 cups	500 mL
Granulated sugar	¼ cup	50 mL
Cornstarch	2 tbsp.	30 mL
Cream cheese, softened	8 oz.	250 g
Granulated sugar	1 cup	250 mL
Whipping cream (or 2 env. topping)	2 cups	500 mL

Crust: Melt butter in saucepan. Stir in crumbs and sugar. Reserve ½ cup and press remaining crumbs into ungreased 9 x 13–inch (22 x 33 cm) pan.

Filling: Combine peaches, juice and water, sugar and cornstarch in saucepan. Heat and stir until it boils and thickens. Cool.

Beat cream cheese with sugar until light and fluffy. Beat cream until stiff. Fold into cheese mixture. Spread ½ onto prepared crust. Spoon thickened peaches over top. Spoon second ½ cheese mixture over as best you can. Sprinkle with reserved crumbs. Chill. Cuts into 15 pieces.

It's a shame that she's losing both her memory and her health. She can't remember the last time she felt well.

PUMPKIN TORTE

Both a refrigerator and a freezer dessert.

CRUST		
Butter or margarine	½ cup	125 mL
Graham cracker crumbs	2 cups	500 mL
Granulated sugar	⅓ cup	75 mL
FILLING		
Cream cheese, softened	8 oz.	250 g
Granulated sugar	¾ cup	175 mL
Eggs	2	2
Unflavored gelatin powder	¼ oz.	7 g
Water	¼ cup	50 mL
Canned pumpkin (without spices)	14 oz.	398 mL
Granulated sugar	½ cup	125 mL
Egg yolks	3	3
Cinnamon	1 tsp.	5 mL
Salt	½ tsp.	2 mL
Milk	½ cup	125 mL
Egg whites	3	3
Granulated sugar	¼ cup	50 mL

Crust: Melt butter in saucepan. Stir in crumbs and sugar. Press into ungreased 9 × 13–inch (22 × 33 cm) pan.

Filling: Beat cream cheese and sugar together well. Beat in 1 egg at a time. Pour over crust. Bake in 325°F (160°C) oven for 20 minutes.

Sprinkle gelatin over water in small bowl. Let stand at least 5 minutes.

Measure next 6 ingredients into saucepan. Heat and stir over medium heat until boiling and thickened. Remove from heat. Stir in softened gelatin until dissolved. Chill until syrupy.

Beat egg whites until soft peaks form. Add sugar gradually, beating until stiff. Fold into pumpkin mixture. Pour over cheese layer. Chill. Serve with sweetened whipped cream. Serves 15.

WHITE SOUFFLÉ

This creamy texture melts in your mouth. The red sauce over white is very dramatic.

Unflavored gelatin powder	¼ oz.	7 g
Water	¼ cup	50 mL
Egg yolks	2	2
Milk	¾ cup	175 mL
Granulated sugar	⅓ cup	75 mL
Egg whites	2	2
Whipping cream (or 1 env. topping)	1 cup	250 mL

Sprinkle gelatin over water in small container. Let stand 5 minutes.

Beat egg yolks with spoon while adding milk gradually. Add sugar. Cook and stir over medium heat until it boils. Remove from heat. Add gelatin mixture. Stir to dissolve. Chill until syrupy.

Beat egg whites until stiff. Using same beaters, beat cream until stiff. Fold egg whites into slightly thickened mixture. Fold in whipped cream. Pour into mold or a pretty bowl. Serve Melba Sauce, page 136, on the side or spoon over unmolded soufflé. Serves 8.

CHOCOLATE SOUFFLÉ: Add 3 tbsp. (50 mL) cocoa to mixture. Garnish with almonds.

Her husband is so careless about his appearance. She hasn't seen him in two months.

PISTACHIO DESSERT

The nutty shortbread crust is such an excellent base for this light dessert. Pretty.

CRUST
All-purpose flour	1 cup	250 mL
Butter or margarine	½ cup	125 mL
Finely chopped pecans	½ cup	125 mL

FILLING
Cream cheese, softened	8 oz.	250 g
Icing (confectioner's) sugar	1 cup	250 mL
Pistachio instant pudding, 6 serving size	1	1
Milk	2 cups	450 mL
Whipping cream (or 1 env. topping)	1 cup	250 mL
Slivered almonds	2 – 3 tbsp.	30 – 50 mL

Crust: Put flour and butter into bowl. Mix until crumbly. Stir in pecans. Press into ungreased 9 × 13-inch (22 × 33 cm) pan. Bake in 350°F (180°C) oven for 15 minutes. Cool.

Filling: Mix cheese and sugar together well. Spread over cooled shortbread crust.

Beat pudding mix with milk. Pour over cheese-sugar layer. Chill a few minutes to firm.

Whip cream until stiff. Spread over pudding layer. Sprinkle with slivered almonds. Serves 15.

Cannibals found they got sick every time they ate a missionary. They just couldn't keep a good man down.

CHERRY CHA CHA

A dessert that requires second helpings. The red cherry sandwiched between marshmallow cream and topped with rich crumbs makes it colorful.

CRUST
Butter or margarine	½ cup	125 mL
Graham cracker crumbs	2 cups	500 mL
Granulated sugar	¼ cup	50 mL

FILLING
Whipping cream (or 2 env. topping)	2 cups	500 mL
Tiny white marshmallows	4 cups	1 L
Cherry pie filling	19 oz.	540 mL

Crust: Melt butter in saucepan over medium heat. Stir in crumbs and sugar. Reserve ⅓ for topping. Press remaining crumbs in ungreased 9 × 13-inch (22 × 33 cm) pan. Bake in 350°F (180°C) oven for 10 minutes. Cool. This works well without baking too.

Filling: Whip cream until stiff. Fold in marshmallows. Spread ½ of this over crumb base.

Spoon cherry pie filling, a small amount at a time, over top, smoothing as best you can. Spread second ½ cream mixture over pie filling. Sprinkle reserved crumbs over all. Chill for several hours before using. Cuts into 12 pieces.

ECONOMICAL CHA CHA: Spread all crumb mixture in 11½ × 17½-inch (30 × 44 cm) pan. No need to bake but allowing to dry for a few hours helps. Beat 6 cups (1.5 L) whipping cream (or use 6 env. topping). Fold in 1 pkg. small white marshmallows or 5 cups (1.25 L). Spoon over crumbs by putting dabs here and there to make for easy spreading. Smooth top. Chill. Before serving, cut into 24 or 30 pieces. Divide cherry pie filling among pieces for topping. Halve recipe to serve 12.

CHOCOLATE CHA CHA: Make the same as for Economical Cha Cha, except add ¾ cup (175 mL) chocolate drink powder along with ¼ cup (60 mL) cocoa to the whipped cream. Omit cherries. Good.

MOCHA CHA CHA: To Chocolate Cha Cha, add 1 tbsp. (15 mL) instant coffee, crushed to a powder. Sprinkle with slivered, sliced or ground almonds. Good too.

PUMPKIN ICE CREAM PIE

The pumpkin–cream layer hides a layer of ice cream.

CRUST		
Butter or margarine	¼ cup	60 mL
Gingersnap crumbs	1½ cups	350 mL
FILLING		
Vanilla ice cream, softened	2 cups	500 mL
Canned pumpkin pie filling (see Note)	1 cup	250 mL
Rum or brandy (optional)	1 tbsp.	15 mL
Egg white	1	1
Whipping cream (or 1 env. topping)	1 cup	250 mL

Crust: Melt butter in saucepan. Stir in crumbs. Press into 9-inch (22 cm) pie plate on 8 × 8-inch (20 × 20 cm) pan. Chill for 15 minutes.

Filling: Spread ice cream in bottom of crust. Freeze while preparing remaining filling.

Mix pumpkin with rum if using.

Beat egg white until stiff. Fold into pumpkin mixture. Beat cream until stiff. Fold into pumpkin mixture. Spread over ice cream layer. Freeze. To serve, let stand 10 to 15 minutes. Cuts into 6 pieces.

Note: To use canned pumpkin, mix 1 cup (250 mL) pumpkin, ½ cup (125 mL) granulated sugar, ¼ tsp. (1 mL) each of cinnamon, nutmeg and ginger and the rum. Proceed with recipe.

1. Baked Alaska page 75.
2. Strawberry Freeze page 74.
3. Watermelon Bombe page 76.
4. Irish Coffee page 149.

APPLE ALASKA BAKE

Unusual in that it is baked in a pie plate.

Peeled and sliced apples	3 cups	750 mL
Brown sugar	½ cup	125 mL
Cinnamon	½ tsp.	2 mL
Water	¼ cup	50 mL
Baked 9 or 10–inch (23 or 25 cm) pie shell	1	1
Vanilla ice cream scoops	6	6
Egg whites	4	4
Cream of tartar	¼ tsp.	1 mL
Brown sugar	½ cup	125 mL

Combine first 4 ingredients in saucepan. Simmer, covered, until cooked. Cool.

In pie shell, spread apple sauce. Arrange ice cream scoops about 1-inch (2.5 cm) in from edge over top of apple filling.

Beat egg whites and cream of tartar together until soft peaks form. Gradually beat in sugar until stiff. Quickly spread over ice cream. Bake in 450°F (230°C) oven for about 3 or 4 minutes until lightly browned. Serves 6 immediately.

DEEP FRIED ICE CREAM

A make-ahead, cook-at-the-last-minute dessert. Easier than you think for a few — not a crowd. Try different colors.

Ice cream, in scoops	1 pt.	500 mL
Graham cracker crumbs, sprinkle of sugar and cinnamon (or use chocolate cookie crumbs or medium coconut)	1 cup	250 mL
Eggs, beaten	2	2
Fat for deep frying		

Scoop ice cream into 4 balls. Put into freezer. Remove and roll in crumbs. Return to freezer. When very firm, dip into beaten eggs and roll in crumbs again. Freeze again.

To serve, deep fry 2 balls at a time in hot fat, 375°F (190°C) for about 10–12 seconds or until browned. Use slotted spoon for easy handling. Serve with or without Deluxe Chocolate Sauce, page 139.

STRAWBERRY FREEZE

A remarkable dessert. Cuts easily and can be served immediately. Keep it on hand. A pretty pink color.

CRUST
Butter or margarine	¾ cup	175 mL
All–purpose flour	1½ cups	375 mL
Brown sugar, packed	½ cup	125 mL
Finely chopped nuts	¾ cup	175 mL

FILLING
Egg whites	2	2
Granulated sugar	¾ cup	175 mL
Frozen sliced strawberries with juice, partly thawed	15 oz.	425 g
Lemon juice	2 tbsp.	30 mL
Whipping cream (or 1 env. topping)	1 cup	250 mL

Crust: Melt butter in medium-size saucepan. Stir in flour, sugar and nuts. Spread in large ungreased baking pan. Bake in 375° (190°C) oven for 15 to 20 minutes, stirring twice, until nicely browned. Remove from oven. Break up any chunks. Scatter ⅔ hot crumbs into ungreased 9 x 13-inch (22 x 33 cm) pan or 10-inch (25 cm) springform pan. Press down.

Filling: In large mixing bowl put egg whites, sugar, strawberries and lemon juice. Beat on high speed until thickened and volume is increased. This will take about 10 minutes.

Beat cream until stiff. Fold into strawberry mixture. Turn into crumb-lined pan. Sprinkle reserved crumbs over top. Cover and freeze overnight or until needed. After first piece is removed, use egg lifter (turner) to take out rest. Makes 15 generous servings.

Pictured on page 71.

BAKED ALASKA

You can have this ready in the freezer and put it in the oven to brown while clearing the table. An impressive dessert and easier to make than you think.

Chocolate cake layer, or brownie layer, round or square	1	1
Block of strawberry ice cream	1	1
Block of chocolate ice cream	1	1
Egg whites	4	4
Cream of tartar	¼ tsp.	1 mL
Granulated sugar	¾ cup	175 mL
Slivered almonds or chopped hazelnuts (optional)	¼ cup	50 mL

A board, covered with aluminum foil makes the best baking pan. Place cake on board. Slice blocks of ice cream in half lengthwise. Cover cake, layering chocolate over strawberry, leaving close to 1 inch (2.5 cm) of cake showing all around outside edge of ice cream. Place in freezer while making meringue.

Beat egg whites and cream of tartar until soft peaks form. Gradually beat in sugar until stiff. Quickly spread over ice cream and cake being sure to cover completely. Sprinkle with nuts if you are using them. (May be frozen and covered at this point.) Bake in 450°F (230°C) oven for about 3 to 4 minutes or until lightly browned. Serves 12.

Variation: Use white cake, jelly roll slice, gingerbread, spice or carrot cake as a base. Use vanilla ice cream.

MOCHA BAKED ALASKA: Use coffee ice cream instead of strawberry. Use brown sugar instead of granulated.

Pictured with brownie layer on page 71.

Note: If making large size, use more egg whites, cream of tartar and sugar.

WATERMELON BOMBE

An easy to make ice cream dessert. A green shell with pink "meat". The seeds are chocolate chips.

Pistachio ice cream or lime ice, softened	1 qt.	1 L
Strawberry ice cream	1 qt.	1 L
Semisweet chocolate chips	½ cup	125 mL

Line melon mold or a bowl with plastic wrap. Using back of spoon, press pistachio ice cream to completely line inside of mold. Freeze 10 minutes.

Stir strawberry ice cream and chocolate chips together. Fill center of mold. Return to freezer. Unmold a few minutes before serving. Makes slices of the coldest watermelon ever.

Pictured on page 71.

BUTTERSCOTCH SQUARES

Almost as soon as this is dished up from the freezer, the sauce starts to ooze over the sides.

CRUST		
Butter or margarine	½ cup	125 mL
All-purpose flour	1 cup	250 mL
Packed brown sugar	¼ cup	50 mL
Chopped pecans	½ cup	125 mL
FILLING		
Jar of butterscotch or caramel syrup (half may be used)	1 cup	250 mL
Vanilla ice cream, in rectangular box for easy cutting	1 qt.	1 L

Crust: Melt butter in saucepan. Stir in flour, sugar and nuts. Spread in large pan. Bake in 350°F (180°C) oven for 10 minutes. Stir well to help even browning. Continue to bake for about 10 minutes more to brown. Stir and cool. Spread ⅔ crumbs in ungreased 8 × 8-inch (20 × 20 cm) pan. Reserve ⅓ for topping.

Filling: Drizzle ½ butterscotch syrup sauce over crumbs. Slice ice cream and layer over top. Drizzle second ½ syrup over ice cream. Scatter reserved crumbs over all. Serves 9.

ICE CREAM TOFFEE SLICE: Use chocolate crumb crust, page 79.

FROZEN LEMON MERINGUE

A spectacular creation ready for those unexpected visits. Lemon at its best.

CRUST		
Butter or margarine	½ cup	125 mL
Graham cracker crumbs	2 cups	500 mL
Brown sugar, packed	⅓ cup	75 mL
FILLING		
Egg yolks	6	6
Sweetened condensed milk	2 – 11 oz.	2 – 300 mL
Frozen lemonade, thawed	12 oz.	341 mL
Lemon juice	2 tbsp.	30 mL
Whipping cream (or 2 env. topping)	2 cups	500 mL
TOPPING		
Egg whites, room temperature	6	6
Granulated sugar	¾ cup	175 mL

Crust: Melt butter in saucepan. Stir in crumbs and sugar. Press into ungreased 9 x 13-inch (22 x 33 cm) pan. Bake in 350°F (180°C) oven for 10 minutes.

Filling: Beat egg yolks until frothy. Beat in condensed milk, condensed lemonade and lemon juice. Beat until thick.

Beat cream until stiff. Fold into milk mixture. Spread over crust.

Topping: Beat egg whites until foamy. Add sugar gradually, beating until stiff. Spread over filling. Place under broiler for only a few seconds. Watch carefully. When golden, remove and cool. Freeze covered. To serve, remove from freezer for 15 to 20 minutes. Serve partially frozen. Serves 15 to 18.

FROZEN MOCHA CHEESECAKE

A worker's dream. Cut a piece or two and pop the rest back into the freezer.

CRUST		
Butter or margarine	½ cup	125 mL
Graham cracker crumbs	1½ cups	375 mL
Granulated sugar	¼ cup	50 mL
Cocoa	¼ cup	50 mL
FILLING		
Cream cheese, softened	8 oz.	250 g
Sweetened condensed milk	11 oz.	300 mL
Chocolate flavored syrup	⅔ cup	150 mL
Instant coffee granules	1 tbsp.	15 mL
Hot water	1 tsp.	5 mL
Whipping cream (or 1 env. topping)	1 cup	250 mL

Crust: Melt butter in medium saucepan over medium heat. Stir in crumbs, sugar and cocoa. Reserve ½ cup (125 mL). Press remaining crumbs into ungreased 9-inch (22 cm) springform pan, bottom and sides.

Filling: Beat cheese until fluffy. Beat in milk and chocolate syrup.

Dissolve coffee in water. Add to cheese mixture.

Beat cream until stiff. Fold into cheese batter. Pour into prepared pan. Scatter reserved crumbs over top. Freeze.

Even if your dreams don't come true, be thankful that your nightmares don't either.

MUD PIE

This recipe has a chocolate topping over the ice cream. If served with hot Deluxe Chocolate Sauce, page 139, you will be acclaimed as having the best Mud Pie ever.

CRUST		
Butter or margarine	½ cup	125 mL
Chocolate wafer crumbs	2 cups	500 mL
FILLING		
Coffee ice cream, softened	4 cups	1 L
TOPPING		
Cocoa	⅓ cup	75 mL
Butter or margarine	3 tbsp.	50 mL
Granulated sugar	⅔ cup	150 mL
Heavy cream or evaporated milk	⅓ cup	75 mL
Vanilla	1 tsp.	5 mL
FINAL GARNISH		
Whipping cream (or 1 env. topping)	1 cup	250 mL
Granulated sugar	1 tbsp.	15 mL
Vanilla	½ tsp.	2 mL
Semisweet chocolate squares	1 – 2	1 – 2

Crust: Melt butter in saucepan. Stir in crumbs. Press in bottom and sides of 9-inch (22 cm) pie plate. Bake in 350°F (180°C) oven for 10 minutes. Cool.

Filling: Spoon ice cream into shell, spreading carefully. Freeze until firm.

Topping: Put all 5 ingredients into saucepan. Heat and stir over medium heat until boiling. Remove from heat. Cool for about 10 minutes, then smooth over ice cream filling. Return to freezer.

Final Garnish: To serve, whip cream, sugar and vanilla until stiff. Spread over top. Garnish with shaved chocolate and sliced almonds. Serves 10.

Note: If you cannot buy coffee ice cream, use vanilla and flavor it with 2 tsp. (10 mL) instant coffee dissolved in 4 tsp. (20 mL) hot water. Mix into softened ice cream.

Note: For a deep pie, double amount of ice cream and use a spring form pan.

CHOCOLATE ICE CREAM ROLL

As long as this is in the freezer, your worries are over. Try various fillings.

Egg whites	4	4
Granulated sugar	¾ cup	175 mL
Egg yolks	4	4
Vanilla	1 tsp.	5 mL
All-purpose flour	6 tbsp.	100 mL
Cocoa	6 tbsp.	100 mL
Baking soda	½ tsp.	2 mL
Salt	¼ tsp.	1 mL
Block of ice cream	½ gal.	2 L

Beat egg whites until very foamy. Add sugar gradually, continuing to beat until stiff peaks will form.

Beat egg yolks and vanilla in a small bowl until thick and lemon colored. Fold into egg whites.

Sift flour, cocoa, soda and salt over top. Fold in. Line greased jelly roll pan, 10 × 15–inch (25 × 38 cm), with waxed paper. Pour batter into pan, smoothing out to corners. Bake in 400°F (200°C) oven for 15 minutes until an inserted toothpick comes out clean. Have tea towel ready with sifted icing (confectioner's) sugar covering it. Turn baked roll out onto towel. Trim crisp edges if any. Roll with towel and cool. Unroll. Layer ice cream in ½–inch (1.25 cm) thick slices over all. Roll again. Freeze until needed. Serves 8–10.

CHOCOLATE LOG: Fill jelly roll with 2 cups (500 mL) cream, whipped, with 1 cup (250 mL) toasted slivered almonds. Roll. Cut a bit off ends to make them smooth. Cover roll with Chocolate Icing. Use 2 rolled center portions of removed ends with Chocolate on top of roll to resemble knots. Ice them also.

CHOCOLATE ICING

Icing (confectioner's) sugar	2 cups	500 mL
Cocoa	6 tbsp.	100 mL
Butter or margarine, softened	¼ cup	60 mL
Prepared coffee or water	2 tbsp.	30 mL

Beat all together adding more liquid or icing sugar if needed for proper spreading consistency.

PEACHES AND ICE CREAM

This is so simple, it is often overlooked. Make only required amount as it doesn't store well.

Fresh peaches, peeled and sliced (or frozen)
Granulated sugar

Vanilla ice cream

Stir peaches with sugar to taste. Chill until about 10 minutes before needed.

In medium sized bowl put about twice as much ice cream as peaches. Add peaches. Stir together. Serve when slightly softened.

BANANA BUTTERSCOTCH

This has to be a must for an easy dessert. A delicious way to use bananas.

Brown sugar, packed	1 cup	250 mL
Butter or margarine	3 tbsp.	60 mL
Cream	2 tbsp.	30 mL
Vanilla	⅛ tsp.	0.5 mL
Medium bananas, sliced	3	3
Whipping cream	½ cup	125 mL
Granulated sugar	1 tsp.	5 mL
Vanilla	½ tsp.	2 mL

Combine sugar, butter, cream and vanilla in saucepan. Bring to boil. Simmer slowly to thicken a bit.

Slice bananas into 4 fruit nappies.

Whip cream, sugar and vanilla until stiff. Spoon hot butterscotch topping over bananas and top with whipped cream. Serves 4.

FRUIT PIZZA

Make your own color arrangement. A sight to behold.

CRUST
All-purpose flour	1¼ cups	275 mL
Brown sugar	⅓ cup	75 mL
Icing (confectioner's) sugar	3 tbsp.	50 mL
Butter, softened	⅔ cup	150 mL

TOPPING
Cream cheese, softened	12 oz.	375 g
Granulated sugar	½ cup	125 mL
Vanilla	1 tsp.	5 mL

Variety of fruit
Whipped cream, for garnish

Crust: Mix all 4 ingredients together in bowl until it forms a ball. Press on bottom of pizza pan. Bake in 350°F (180°C) oven for about 10 to 15 minutes or until golden brown. Cool.

Topping: Beat cheese, sugar and vanilla together. Spread over crust.

Arrange fruit in pattern of your choice over top. Glaze fruit. Garnish around edge with whipped cream if desired.

APRICOT GLAZE: Mix ¼ cup (60 mL) apricot jam or orange marmalade with 1 tbsp. (15 mL) water. Rub through sieve.

Pictured on page 89.

PEARS HÉLÈNE

Pears and ice cream smothered in chocolate sauce. More impressive yet is to dip pears in chocolate coating.

Vanilla ice cream
Canned pear halves (or fresh, cooked)
Deluxe chocolate sauce, page 139, heated

Scoop or spoon ice cream into serving dishes. Place pear half, cut side down, on top. Use 2 smaller halves depending on size of serving desired. Spoon hot sauce over all. Top with whipped cream. Garnish with nuts or a cherry if desired.

Variation: Serve with Melba Sauce, page 136, instead of chocolate.

BAKED APPLES

Make as many or as few as needed. Always good.

Cooking apples	4	4
Brown sugar		
Butter or margarine	2 tsp.	10 mL

Remove core from center of apples. Place in baking pan. Pack cavities with brown sugar. Put a dab of butter on top of each sugar stuffing. For a bit of extra syrup when cooked, or if apples appear a bit dry, add ¼ cup (50 mL) water and ⅓ cup (75 mL) brown sugar to pan. Bake in 350°F (180°C) oven for about 40 minutes or until apples are tender. Serve in fruit nappie. Spoon sauce over top. Serve with cream or milk.

BAKED MINCEMEAT APPLES: Remove apples from oven about half way through baking. Spoon mincemeat into cavities. Continue baking until tender. Good with ice cream.

Variation: Add cinnamon to sugar for stuffing if desired.

STRAWBERRIES ROMANOFF

Definitely for fresh strawberries only. Quick, easy and very impressive.

Ripe strawberries, medium-size	1 qt.	1.25 L
Icing (confectioner's) sugar	½ cup	125 mL
Orange juice	½ cup	125 mL
Curaçao (or Grand Marnier or Cointreau)	½ cup	125 mL
Whipping cream	1 cup	250 mL
Granulated sugar	1 tbsp.	15 mL
Curaçao (or Grand Marnier or Cointreau)	1 tsp.	5 mL

Combine cleaned whole strawberries, icing sugar, orange juice and curaçao in bowl. Chill, covered, for several hours, turning or stirring occasionally. Divide fruit and juice among 8 champagne glasses, sherbets or other containers.

Whip cream and granulated sugar together until stiff. Add curaçao for flavoring. Spoon over berries. Serves 8.

Variation: Granulated sugar may be substituted for the icing sugar. Other fresh fruit may be used such as peaches, apricots, blueberries.

FRUIT COMPOTE

A refreshing summer dessert that is convenient for a crowd. Easy to adjust for any number of guests.

Cantaloupe balls or pieces
Honeydew balls or pieces
Watermelon balls or pieces
Seedless grapes
Mandarin oranges, drained
Pineapple chunks
Apple wedges, unpeeled
Strawberries
Kiwifruit slices
Orange wedges
Banana slices

Combine fruit in large container. All fruit listed need not be used but using all colors makes a better appearing bowl. Have a bowl of sauce, topping or dip beside fruit to spoon over top each serving.

EASY FRUIT SAUCE

Yogurt or sour cream	1 cup	250 mL
Brown sugar	2 tbsp.	30 mL
Grated orange peel	1 tsp.	5 mL

Stir together well. Use as a topping or dip.

FRUIT DRESSING

All-purpose flour	2 tbsp.	30 mL
Granulated sugar	½ cup	125 mL
Beaten egg	1	1
Orange juice	½ cup	125 mL
Pineapple juice	½ cup	125 mL
Butter or margarine	1 tbsp.	15 mL
Whipping cream (or 1 env. topping)	1 cup	250 mL

In top of double boiler stir flour and sugar together well. Stir in beaten egg. Add juices. Cook over boiling water stirring frequently until thickened. Stir in butter. Cool.

Whip cream until stiff. Fold into cooled dressing. Spoon over individual servings of salad.

FRUIT SAUCE

Cream cheese, softened	8 oz.	250 g
Granulated sugar, syrup or honey	¼ cup	50 mL
Orange juice	½ cup	125 mL

Beat all ingredients together. Add more orange juice if needed to thin sauce a bit more, although there will be some juice on the fruit so don't make it too thin. Really good. Makes a scant 2 cups (450 mL).

CHERRIES JUBILEE

So simple yet so elegant. A snap with pie filling.

Cherry pie filling	19 oz.	540 mL
Brandy	¼ cup	50 mL
Scoops of ice cream in dishes		

Put cherries in wide container to heat such as a chafing dish or saucepan. Have hot before proceeding.

Put brandy into small cup. Set in very hot water to warm brandy. Light with match. Pour over warm cherries.

Spoon over ice cream while still flaming or stir until flames subside. Makes 2½ cups (375 mL) sauce.

Note: Dark canned cherries may be used. Stir 2 tbsp. (30 mL) cornstarch into juice from 2 – 14 oz. (2 – 398 mL) cans. Add ¼ cup (50 mL) granulated sugar and 2 tsp. (10 mL) lemon juice. Stir and cook until boiling and thickened. Combine with cherries.

Note: Brandy may be heated in small saucepan. If you watch closely, you will see vapor begin to rise. Light with match at that point. If allowed to lose too much vapor, it won't flame enough.

CHOCOLATE DIPPED STRAWBERRIES

This fabulous fruit is best prepared just a few hours before serving.

Semisweet chocolate chips	⅔ cup	150 mL
Parowax (cut bits to measure)	1 tbsp.	15 mL
Fresh strawberries	1 qt.	1.25 L

Heat chips and wax in top of double boiler or pan over hot water. Stir until smooth. Remove from heat but return as chocolate cools.

Dip strawberries to coat bottom ⅔. Drain for a few seconds over chocolate mixture then place on stem end to cool or lay them on waxed paper. Chill until ready to serve. Plan to have at room temperature about 1 hour for serving.

CHOCOLATE DIPPED FRUIT: Use mixture to dip Mandarin orange slices, pineapple chunks, tiny clusters of 2-3 seedless grapes, and maraschino cherries. The drier the fruit, the better the results.

FRUIT TRAY: Arrange Chocolate Dipped Strawberries and Fruit on tray with bunches of grapes, banana slices dipped in lemon juice and rolled toasted coconut (put medium coconut in 350°F (180°C) oven for 5-10 minutes, stirring often). Set out 1 or 2 fruit dips.

Variation: For an extra, as well as for those few who don't care for chocolate, dip some fruit in melted almond bark.

CARAMEL FRUIT DIP

Sour cream	1 cup	250 mL
Brown sugar	1 tbsp.	15 mL
Kahlua	1 tbsp.	15 mL

Stir together. If you prefer to omit kahlua, add more brown sugar to taste. Make a good supply. It vanishes in no time. Makes 1 cup (250 mL).

EASY FRUIT DIP

Plain yogurt	1 cup	250 mL
Icing (confectioner's) sugar	3 tbsp.	50 mL
Grated lemon peel	½ tsp.	2 mL

Combine all ingredients. A bit less lemon peel may be used. This makes a yummy dip for any fruit. Makes 1 cup (250 mL).

PEACH MELBA

A classic made quickly with a jam sauce. This is also excellent with Melba Sauce.

Raspberry jam	⅔ cup	150 mL
Hot water	2 tbsp.	30 mL
Lemon juice	½ tsp.	2 mL
Scoops of ice cream	6	6
Sliced peaches, drained	14 oz.	398 mL

Combine jam, water and lemon juice. Stir. Strain to remove seeds.

Put ice cream into sherbets. Arrange peach slices over top. Spoon raspberry mixture over top. Serve with a cookie wafer if desired. Peach halves may be used in place of sliced. Try the Melba sauce, page 136.

FRUIT CARAMEL

A tasty, different way to serve fruit.

Mixed canned fruit, drained, or soft fresh fruit	5 cups	1.25 L
Sour cream	1 cup	250 mL
Cream cheese, softened	8 oz.	250 g
Orange flavored liqueur (optional)	2 tbsp.	30 mL
Granulated sugar	2 tbsp.	30 mL
Packed brown sugar	½ cup	125 mL

Spread fruit in 8 × 8–inch (20 × 20 cm) pan.

Beat sour cream and cream cheese until smooth. Mix in liqueur and sugar. Spread over fruit.

Sift brown sugar over top, covering evenly. Broil 6 inches (15 cm) from heat until sugar starts to melt. Watch so it doesn't scorch. Serves 8.

INSTANT FRUIT CARAMEL: Lay pear halves or peach halves in casserole or pan. Cover with sour cream, amount is optional and depends on how many fruit halves used. Sprinkle with a good cover of brown sugar. Broil until sugar melts. Don't scorch.

BRANDIED PEACHES

This can be made in a jiffy. Especially good when you have no idea how many people will want dessert. It can be prepared as served.

Canned peaches with juice	2 – 14 oz.	2 – 398 mL
Brown sugar, packed	⅔ cup	150 mL
Butter or margarine	2 tbsp.	30 mL
Cinnamon	¼ tsp.	1 mL
Lemon juice	1 tsp.	5 mL
Brandy flavoring (or ¼ cup, 50 mL brandy)	1 tsp.	5 mL
Almond flavoring (optional)	¼ tsp.	1 mL
Vanilla ice cream		

Cut up peaches into slices or pieces and put into saucepan along with juice. Add sugar, butter, cinnamon, lemon juice, brandy flavoring and almond if using. Heat over medium heat until boiling. Simmer 5 minutes. Keep hot until ready to serve or make ahead and heat when needed.

Put scoops of ice cream into dishes. Ladle brandied peaches over top. Serves 12.

1. Fruit Pizza page 82.
2. Pecan Bites page 145.

SAUCED BANANAS

Make the sauce ahead of time. Keep it warm or warm it when ready to serve. Be prepared for seconds.

Butter or margarine	⅓ cup	75 mL
Brown sugar, packed	⅓ cup	75 mL
Cinnamon	½ tsp.	2 mL
Dash of nutmeg		
Light cream	¼ cup	50 mL
Rum (or water plus ½ tsp., 2 mL, rum flavoring)	2 tbsp.	30 mL
Vanilla or butterscotch-ripple ice cream		
Bananas, sliced		

Mix first 6 ingredients in saucepan. Heat and stir to combine well.

Put ice cream into dishes. Top with banana slices. Spoon hot sauce over all. Makes ⅔ cup (150 mL).

FROSTY CLOUDS

The name says it all. Everyone will want your ice cream recipe — but it isn't. Great freezer food.

Granulated sugar	½ cup	125 mL
Water	3 tbsp.	50 mL
Egg whites	2	2
Whipping cream	½ cup	125 mL
Vanilla	½ tsp.	2 mL
Frozen raspberries or strawberries, thawed, or cherry pie filling or other fruit		

Measure sugar and water into small saucepan. Cook and stir over medium heat until a thread forms when spoon is lifted. Remove from heat.

Beat egg whites until stiff. Slowly pour sugar-water mixture into whites while beating continuously until light-colored and cool.

Whip cream and vanilla until stiff. Fold into egg white mixture. Spoon into paper cups or muffin tins, rounding tops nicely. Freeze. Cover to store. To serve, unmold and add your favorite fruit. Makes 10.

DACQUOISE

These meringues are filled with a mocha butter filling. A French specialty.

MERINGUE		
Egg whites, room temperature	6	6
Cream of tartar	¼ tsp.	1 mL
Granulated sugar	¾ cup	175 mL
Ground or crushed almonds	¾ cup	175 mL
Cocoa	¼ cup	60 mL
Cornstarch	1 tbsp.	15 mL
CREAMED FILLING		
Egg yolks	6	6
Granulated sugar	¾ cup	175 mL
Butter or margarine, softened	1 cup	225 mL
Instant coffee granules, crushed to a powder	1 tbsp.	15 mL
Whipping cream	1 cup	250 mL
Granulated sugar	1 tbsp.	15 mL
Vanilla	½ tsp.	2 mL

Meringue: Beat egg whites and cream of tartar until soft peaks form. Add sugar, 1 tbsp. (15 mL) at a time, beating until very stiff.

Stir nuts, cocoa and cornstarch together. Fold into beaten whites. Spread on very lightly greased foil-lined cookie sheets in 2 circles, 9 inches (23 cm) in diameter. Bake in 250°F (130°C) oven for about 50 minutes until dry and fairly firm. Allow to cool before removing foil.

Creamed Filling: Beat egg yolks until thick and light. Beat in sugar until fluffy. Add butter ¼ at a time, beating well. Beat in instant coffee. Beat well. Spread ⅔ over 1 meringue layer. Cover with second layer. Spread or pipe remaining butter mixture on outside 2 inches (5 cm).

Whip cream, sugar and vanilla until stiff. Fill center of top meringue and frost sides. Serve within 2 or 3 hours of assembling to 12 guests.

Variation: Omit cocoa from Meringue and add it to the Creamed Filling. Like another dessert.

CLOUD NINE

This meringue is filled with a most luscious chocolate filling.

MERINGUE
Egg whites, room temperature	2	2
Cream of tartar	⅛ tsp.	0.5 mL
Granulated sugar	½ cup	125 mL
Finely chopped pecans	½ cup	125 mL

FILLING
Semisweet chocolate chips	1⅓ cups	300 mL
Water	3 tbsp.	50 mL
Whipping cream (or 1 env. topping)	1 cup	250 mL

Meringue: Beat egg whites and cream of tartar until soft peaks form. Gradually beat in sugar, beating until very stiff and glossy.

Fold in nuts. Spread on foil-lined cookie sheet in an 8-inch (20 cm) circle. Make center about ½-inch (2.5 cm) thick with edges about 1¾-inches (4.5 cm) high. Bake in 275°F (140°C) oven for 1 hour. Turn off oven. Leave meringue in oven for 1½ hours. Cool and transfer to plate.

Filling: Melt chips and water in heavy saucepan over low heat, stirring. Cool.

Whip cream until stiff. Fold chocolate into cream. Pile into meringue shell. Chill 2 or 3 hours before serving. Rich enough to serve 8.

Pictured on page 107.

We are strictly all male workers in this bookkeeping office. There is no accounting for women.

CHOCOLATE MERINGUE TORTE

Brown sugar meringues layered with a chocolate mixture. Perfectly decadent! Very rich.

MERINGUE		
Egg whites, room temperature	4	4
Cream of tartar	¼ tsp.	1 mL
Salt	¼ tsp.	1 mL
Packed brown sugar	1 cup	250 mL
FILLING		
Cream cheese, softened	8 oz.	250 g
Milk	2 tbsp.	30 mL
Granulated sugar	½ cup	125 mL
Semisweet chocolate chips	1 cup	250 mL
Whipping cream (or 1 env. topping)	1 cup	250 mL

Meringue: Beat egg whites, cream of tartar and salt until soft peaks form. Add brown sugar gradually, beating until very stiff. Outline 3 circles, 8 inches (20 cm) each, on very lightly greased foil-lined cookie sheets. Spread meringue, smoothing tops. Bake in 275°F (140°C) oven for about 50 minutes until dry and fairly firm to touch. Cool before removing foil. removing foil.

Filling: Beat cheese, milk and granulated sugar together well.

Melt chips over low heat. Cool. Beat into cheese mixture.

Whip cream until stiff. Fold into chocolate-cheese mixture. Spread between layers, saving enough to frost top layer and sides. Chill 8 hours or overnight. Cut into 8 or 10 small wedges.

Pictured on page 107.

Is it possible for a tree surgeon to have six branch offices?

LEMON TORTE

Any lemon lover won't be able to top this for natural lemon goodness.

MERINGUE

Egg whites, room temperature	3	3
Almond flavoring	1 tsp.	5 mL
Cream of tartar	¼ tsp.	1 mL
Baking powder	1 tsp.	5 mL
Granulated sugar	1 cup	250 mL
Graham cracker crumbs	½ cup	125 mL
Finely chopped pecans	1 cup	250 mL

Beat egg whites, flavoring, cream of tartar and baking powder until soft peaks form. Add sugar gradually, beating until stiff.

Fold in cracker crumbs and nuts. Spread in greased 10-inch (25 cm) pie plate, spreading well up the sides. Bake in 300°F (150°C) oven for about 45 minutes until dry. Fill with lemon filling.

LEMON FILLING

Egg yolks	3	3
Granulated sugar	½ cup	125 mL
Lemon juice	3 tbsp.	50 mL
Grated lemon rind	1 tsp.	5 mL
Whipping cream (or 1 env. topping)	1 cup	250 mL

Mix first 4 ingredients together in heavy saucepan. Heat and stir until thickened. Cool.

Whip cream until stiff. Fold into cooled mixture. Fill meringue shell.

Note: Crumbs from soda crackers, or other types such as Ritz, may be used instead of Graham cracker crumbs.

Pictured on page 107.

PAVLOVA

A wonderful treat from "down under". Traditionally served with kiwifruit, any other fruit may be arranged on top also. The center has a creamy marshmallow–like texture.

MERINGUE

Egg whites, room temperature	4	4
Granulated sugar	1 cup	250 mL
Cornstarch	1 tsp.	5 mL
Vinegar	1 tsp.	5 mL
Vanilla	1 tsp.	5 mL

Beat egg whites until soft peaks form. Add sugar and cornstarch gradually, beating until stiff. Beat in vinegar and vanilla. When rubbing between fingers, there should be no grainy feel to the whites. Outline a foil–lined cookie sheet in a 9–inch (22 cm) circle. Spread meringue in circle. Bake in 250°F (130°C) oven for about 50 to 60 minutes. Turn off heat and allow meringue to stand in oven for at least 1 hour. Cool before removing foil. Cover with topping.

TOPPING

Whipping cream	1 cup	250 mL
Granulated sugar	2 tbsp.	30 mL
Vanilla	1 tsp.	5 mL
Kiwifruit, peeled and sliced or strawberries, sliced or peaches, peeled and sliced, or combination of fruit	2 cups	500 mL

Whip cream, sugar and vanilla until stiff. Spread over top of meringue layer.

Arrange fruit of your choice in an attractive pattern over top. Glaze fruit. Chill until ready to serve. May be made a day ahead with whipped cream and fruit topping added the day it is needed. May also be frozen. Serves 8 to 10.

SIMPLE FRUIT GLAZE: Mix ¼ cup (60 mL) granulated sugar, ¼ cup (60 mL) water and 1½ tsp. (7 mL) cornstarch in saucepan. Bring to boil to thicken. Cool. Paint fruit to seal and shine.

APPLE JELLY GLAZE: Heat ¼ cup (60 mL) light–colored apple or crabapple jelly with 1 tbsp. (15 mL) water. Cool. Dab on fruit.

STRAWBERRY GLAZE: Heat ¼ cup (60 mL) strawberry jelly with 1 tbsp. (15 mL) water. Cool. Brush on fruit.

BOCCONNE DOLCE

An Italian favorite that made Sardi's famous. Meringue layers with chocolate, strawberries and cream.

MERINGUE		
Egg whites, room temperature	6	6
Cream of tartar	¼ tsp.	1 mL
Granulated sugar	1½ cups	350 mL
FILLING		
Semisweet chocolate chips	1 cup	250 mL
Water	3 tbsp.	50 mL
Whipping cream	3 cups	750 mL
Granulated sugar	5 tbsp.	75 mL
Vanilla	2 tsp.	10 mL
Fresh strawberries, sliced lengthwise — save a few for garnish	3 cups	750 mL

Meringue: Beat egg whites and cream of tartar until soft peaks form. Beat in sugar gradually, beating until stiff and glossy. Line 3 round 8-inch (20 cm) pans with foil or outline 3 circles, 8-inch (20 cm), on foil-lined cookie sheets. Very lightly grease the foil. Divide and spread the meringue evenly among the pans. Bake in 250°F (130°C) oven for about 45 minutes until dry and crispy firm. Cool on racks. Peel off foil.

Filling: In heavy saucepan, melt chips with water over low heat. Spread over 2 meringue shells.

Whip cream, sugar and vanilla until stiff. Spread over all 3 meringue layers. Place 1 layer with chocolate on serving plate. Spoon ½ strawberries over top. Place second layer with chocolate over first on plate. Spoon second ½ strawberries over top. Add third layer. Garnish with whole berries. Chill 4 to 5 hours before serving. Serves 8.

Pictured on cover.

STRAWBERRY MERINGUE SHORTCAKE: Beat first 3 ingredients only. Shape into several smaller meringues with raised sides. To serve, fill with sweetened strawberries and top with whipped cream.

CHOCOLATE PIE

A fluffy top on a chewy crust. Really good.

MERINGUE		
Egg whites, room temperature	3	3
Cream of tartar	¼ tsp.	1 mL
Granulated sugar	¾ cup	175 mL
Chocolate wafer crumbs	¾ cup	175 mL
Finely chopped walnuts	½ cup	125 mL
FILLING		
Whipping cream (or 1 env. topping)	1 cup	250 mL
Granulated sugar	1 tbsp.	15 mL
Vanilla	1 tsp.	5 mL
Unsweetened or semisweet chocolate square	1	1

Meringue: Beat egg whites and cream of tartar until soft peaks form. Add sugar gradually, beating until stiff.

Fold in chocolate crumbs and nuts. Spread into greased 9–inch (22 cm) pie plate. Bake in 325°F (160°C) oven for 35 minutes. Cool.

Filling: Whip cream, sugar and vanilla until stiff. Spread over top. Shave chocolate over cream. Chill at least 3 hours before serving. Cuts into 6 pieces.

Pictured on page 107.

BLACK FOREST CRÊPES

Just a few minutes and your dessert is ready. Having a supply of crêpes in the freezer really helps.

Chocolate crêpes (page 104)		
Kirsch or sherry (optional)		
Cherry pie filling (cold or hot)	19 oz.	540 mL
Granulated sugar	¼ cup	50 mL
Nutmeg	⅛ tsp.	0.5 mL
Sweetened whipped cream		

Sprinkle crêpes with kirsch or sherry.

Mix cherry pie filling, sugar and nutmeg together. Spoon about 2 tbsp. (30 mL) close to 1 side of crêpe. Roll. Allow 2 per serving. Lay on plate.

Spoon sweetened whipped cream over top.

APPLE DUMPLINGS

These pastry dumplings are a treat to eat hot or cold, with or without a sauce.

Pie crust, your own or a mix (page 105)

Cooking apples	6	6
Brown sugar, packed	¾ cup	175 mL
Cinnamon	½ tsp.	2 mL

Roll pie crust. Cut in squares large enough to completely encase apple.

Peel apples and remove cores. Place on pastry. Mix brown sugar and cinnamon together. Stuff apples. Moisten edges of pastry, gather to the top and pinch to seal. Arrange in baking pan. Bake at 350°F (180°C) oven for about 1 hour. Serve hot or cold with Brown Sugar Sauce, page 142, Vanilla Pudding Sauce, page 142, cream or ice cream.

Pictured on page 125.

APPLE OAT SQUARES

A creamy apple dessert, good warm or cold. Quite thin so it takes a large pan to make 10 servings.

CRUST

Butter or margarine	½ cup	125 mL
All-purpose flour	¾ cup	175 mL
Rolled oats	¾ cup	175 mL

FILLING

Sweetened condensed milk	11 oz.	300 mL
Sour cream	1 cup	250 mL
Peeled and sliced apples, cherries, blueberries or peaches	1 cup	250 mL
Finely chopped nuts	½ cup	125 mL
Cinnamon sprinkle		

Crust: Melt butter in medium saucepan. Stir in flour and rolled oats. Press into ungreased 9 x 13-inch (22 x 33 cm) pan.

Filling: Mix condensed milk with sour cream. Spread over crust.

Arrange apples over top. Scatter nuts over followed by a sprinkle of cinnamon. Bake in 350°F (180°C) oven for 25 to 30 minutes. Serve warm or cold with ice cream or whipped cream. Cuts into 10 pieces.

DANISH APPLE BARS

Try this — you will agree it is good, good, good.

CRUST
All-purpose flour	2½ cups	625 mL
Salt	1 tsp.	5 mL
Butter or margarine	1 cup	250 mL
Egg yolk	1	1
Milk to make	½ cup	125 mL

FILLING
Crushed corn flakes	1 cup	250 mL
Large apples, peeled and sliced	4	4
Granulated sugar	1 cup	250 mL
Cinnamon	1 tsp.	5 mL
Egg white	1	1

Crust: Measure flour, salt and butter into bowl. Cut in butter until crumbly.

Using fork, beat yolk with small amount of milk in measuring cup. Add milk to make ½ cup (125 mL). Add to flour mixture. Mix and shape into 2 equal balls. Roll 1 ball into 12 x 17-inch (30 x 42 cm) size. Put into 10 x 15-inch (25 x 38 cm) jelly roll pan pressing up sides.

Filling: Scatter corn flake crumbs over crust. Arrange apples slices over crumbs. Cover with sugar and cinnamon. Roll remaining pastry. Moisten bottom crust edges. Cover with pastry and seal. Cut slits in top crust.

Beat egg white stiff. Brush over crust. Bake in 375°F (190°C) oven for about 35 minutes until browned and apples are tender. Glaze while warm.

GLAZE
Icing (confectioner's) sugar	1 cup	225 mL
Water	1 tbsp.	15 mL
Vanilla	½ tsp.	2 mL

Beat all together. Spread over warm crust. Cuts into 15 pieces.

APPLE PAN DOWDY

These scrumptious sauced dumplings are so easy to make. You will be reminded of time long passed. Could this be nostalgia?

All-purpose flour	2 cups	450 mL
Baking powder	2 tsp.	10 mL
Salt	1 tsp.	5 mL
Butter or margarine	½ cup	125 mL
Milk	⅔ cup	150 mL
Cinnamon sprinkle		
Apples, peeled and grated	6	6
Granulated sugar	6 tbsp.	100 mL
Cinnamon sprinkle		
SAUCE		
Brown sugar, packed	1 cup	250 mL
Hot water	2 cups	500 mL
Butter or margarine	1 tbsp.	15 mL
Vanilla	1 tsp.	5 mL

Put flour, baking powder and salt into bowl. Cut in butter until crumbly.

Add milk and mix to form into 2 balls. Roll each into a rectangular shape, 7 x 12 inches (18 x 30 cm).

Sprinkle lightly with cinnamon. Cover with apple. Sprinkle sugar over apple followed by another sprinkle of cinnamon. Starting with the long side, roll like a jelly roll. Cut into 1½ inch (4 cm) pieces. Stand on end (not cut side) in deep casserole.

Sauce: Mix brown sugar, water, butter and vanilla together. Pour over slices. Bake in 350°F (180°C) oven for about 40 minutes. Makes 16 pieces.

Note: To place cut side down, use large baking pan with sides.

Of course you know that a musician cleans his tuba with a tuba toothpaste.

FLAPPER PIE

The best — an absolute dream.

CRUST
Butter or margarine	¼ cup	60 mL
Graham cracker crumbs	1⅓ cups	300 mL
Brown sugar	¼ cup	50 mL

FILLING
Milk	2 cups	450 mL
Egg yolks	3	3
Cornstarch	3 tbsp.	50 mL
Granulated sugar	¼ cup	60 mL
Vanilla	1 tsp.	5 mL
Salt	¼ tsp.	1 mL

MERINGUE
Egg whites, room temperature	3	3
Cream of tartar	¼ tsp.	1 mL
Granulated sugar	3 tbsp.	50 mL

Crust: Melt butter in saucepan over medium heat. Stir in crumbs and sugar. Press into 9-inch (22 cm) pie plate. Bake in 350°F (180°C) oven for 10 minutes.

Filling: Heat milk in heavy pot over medium heat until boiling.

Mix egg yolks, cornstarch, sugar and vanilla together. Stir into milk, stirring until it returns to boiling and thickens. Pour into shell.

Meringue: Beat egg whites and cream of tartar until soft peaks form. Beat in sugar gradually until stiff. Pile onto filling, spreading to edge, covering filling completely. Bake in 400°F (200°C) oven for 5 to 8 minutes until golden. Chill. Serves 6.

Note: If eggs are in short supply, 2 may be used instead of 3.

Cannibals make good fathers. They just want an edible young man for their daughter.

CREAM PUFFS

Large or small, everyone likes them. Try all the variations as well.

Boiling water	1 cup	250 mL
Butter or margarine	½ cup	125 mL
Salt	¼ tsp.	1 mL
All-purpose flour	1 cup	250 mL
Eggs	4	4
Whipped cream		

Combine water, butter and salt in medium saucepan. Stir to melt butter. Bring to a boil.

Add flour all at once. Stir vigorously until it forms a ball and pulls away from sides of pan. Remove from heat.

Add eggs, one at a time, beating thoroughly after each is added. Drop by spoonfuls onto greased baking sheet leaving room for expansion. Bake in 425°F (220°C) oven for 30 minutes. They should look dry with no beads of moisture showing. Cool on rack. When cool, cut top almost off, fill with flavored and sweetened whipped cream. Makes 12 large puffs.

PROFITEROLES: Make tiny puffs. Fill with sweetened whipped cream, custard or ice cream. Pile puffs onto each plate, (or use 1 extra large plate), in the shape of a pyramid. Pour sauce over top, allowing it to run down the sides. Use Deluxe Chocolate Sauce, page 139.

BUTTERSCOTCH PUFFS: Make as Profiteroles but drizzle with Butterscotch Sauce, page 139.

MELBA PUFFS: Make as Profiteroles but drizzle with Melba Sauce, page 136.

Pictured on page 125.

CHOCOLATE ECLAIRS: Shape pastry into oblong shapes before baking. Allow 10 to 15 minutes more baking time. Fill with Chocolate Chantilly, page 147, or with Custard Sauce, page 133, or Blanc Mange, page 135. Glaze with 1 cup (250 mL) icing (confectioner's) sugar, ¼ cup (50 mL) cocoa, 3 tbsp. (50 mL) butter or margarine, and 3 tbsp. (50 mL) hot coffee or water. Beat well, adjusting liquid so glaze is soft enough to dip tops of eclairs or spread easily with knife. Tops may be dipped into melted semisweet chocolate chips — top notch!

CRÊPES

So many variations can be made from basic crêpes. They freeze so well.

Eggs	4	4
Milk	1 cup	250 mL
Water	1 cup	250 mL
All-purpose flour	2 cups	500 mL
Cooking oil	4 tbsp.	60 mL
Granulated sugar	1 tsp.	5 mL
Salt	¼ tsp.	1 mL

Beat eggs in large bowl until frothy. Add rest of ingredients. Beat smooth. Cover and store in refrigerator overnight or at least a few hours. Add milk before cooking if too thick. Pour 2 tbsp. (30 mL) in greased hot crêpe pan. Tip pan to swirl batter all over pan bottom. Remove when underside is lightly browned. Stack with waxed paper between each crêpe. Secure in plastic bag to store in freezer. Use as needed. Makes 24 crêpes.

CHOCOLATE CRÊPES: Take out 2 tbsp. (30 mL) flour and add 2 tbsp. (30 mL) cocoa.

CHOCOLATE SAUCED CRÊPES: Cut vanilla (or strawberry or chocolate) ice cream about 1 x 1 x 4 inches long (2.5 x 2.5 x 15 cm long) and lay on edge of unbrowned side of crêpe. Roll. Allow 2 crêpes per serving. Spoon hot Deluxe Chocolate Sauce, page 139, over top.

STRAWBERRY CRÊPES: Roll as for Chocolate Sauced Crêpes. Spoon warm Strawberry Sauce, page 23, over top.

BLUEBERRY CRÊPES: Roll as for Chocolate Sauced Crêpes. Spoon warm Blueberry Sauce, page 136, over top.

Pictured on page 125.

BUTTERSCOTCH CRÊPES: Roll as for Chocolate Sauced Crêpes. Spoon warm Butterscotch Sauce, page 139, over top.

APRICOT CRÊPES: Roll as for Chocolate Sauced Crêpes, using vanilla ice cream. Spoon warm Apricot Sauce, page 139, over top.

STRAWBERRY CREAM CRÊPES

Crêpes spread with a cream cheese mixture and topped with strawberries.

Cream cheese, softened	8 oz.	250 g
Granulated sugar	¼ cup	50 mL
Sour cream	1 cup	250 mL
Prepared crêpes	12	12
Strawberries, sliced	2 cups	500 mL
Granulated sugar	¼ cup	50 mL

Beat cream cheese, first amount of sugar and sour cream well.

Spread cheese mixture over unbrowned sides of crêpes. Roll. Allow 2 per serving.

Stir strawberries and sugar together. Spoon over crêpes. Serves 6

PIE CRUST PASTRY

Makes a tender, flaky pie crust.

All-purpose flour	5 cups	1.25 L
Salt	2 tsp.	10 mL
Baking powder	1 tsp.	5 mL
Brown sugar	3 tbsp.	45 mL
Lard, room temperature	1 lb.	454 g
Egg	1	1
Vinegar	2 tbsp.	30 mL
Add cold water to make	1 cup	225 mL

Measure flour, salt, baking powder and brown sugar into large bowl. Stir to distribute all ingredients.

Add lard. Cut into pieces with knife. With pastry cutter, cut in lard until whole mixture is crumbly and feels moist.

Break egg into measuring cup. Beat well with fork. Add vinegar. Add cold water to measure 1 cup (225 mL). Pour slowly over flour mixture stirring with fork to distribute. With hands, work until it will hold together. Divide into 4 equal parts. Each part is sufficient for a 2-crust, 9-inch (22 cm) pie. Wrap in plastic and store in refrigerator for 1 or 2 weeks. Store in freezer to have a continuing supply.

BERRY TORTE

Shortbread cookie layers make an excellent foundation for fresh fruit and cream.

PASTRY LAYERS
All–purpose flour	4 cups	1 L
Brown sugar, packed	⅓ cup	75 mL
Icing (confectioner's) sugar	⅓ cup	75 mL
Butter, softened (not margarine)	2 cups	500 mL

FILLING
Whipping cream	2 cups	500 mL
Granulated sugar	¼ cup	50 mL
Vanilla	1 tsp.	5 mL
Fresh peaches, strawberries or raspberries	2 cups	500 mL
Butterscotch sauce (optional)		

Pastry Layers: Combine all together in bowl. Work together until it will form a ball. Divide into 4 equal balls. Roll each to ¼ inch (.75 cm) thickness. Place on ungreased baking sheets. Prick with fork. Bake in 325°F (160°C) oven for about 15 minutes or until lightly browned.

Filling: Beat cream, sugar and vanilla until stiff. Fold in fruit. Spread between layers and on top. Garnish with fresh fruit. Drizzle with Butterscotch Sauce, page 139, or serve as is. Chill for 2 or 3 hours before serving. Cuts into 10 wedges.

1. Cloud Nine page 93.
2. Chocolate Pie page 98.
3. Chocolate Meringue Torte page 94.
4. Lemon Torte page 95.

RAINBOW SQUARES

Great for an afternoon tea. The glistening cherry and pineapple filling rests on a shortbread base and is topped with meringue.

CRUST		
All-purpose flour	2 cups	500 mL
Granulated sugar	2 tbsp.	30 mL
Butter or margarine	1 cup	250 mL
FILLING		
Crushed pineapple with juice	19 oz.	540 mL
Granulated sugar	½ cup	125 mL
Cornstarch	3 tbsp.	50 mL
Maraschino cherries with juice, cut up	4 oz.	125 mL
Almond flavoring	1 tsp.	5 mL
Egg whites	2	2
Granulated sugar	2 tbsp.	30 mL
Vanilla	1 tsp.	5 mL
Coconut	¼ cup	50 mL

Crust: Mix flour, first amount of sugar and butter together until crumbly. Press into ungreased 9 x 13-inch (22 x 33 cm) pan. Bake in 350°F (180°C) oven for 15 minutes.

Filling: Put first 5 ingredients into saucepan. Heat and stir over medium heat until it boils and thickens. Pour over shortbread base. Cool.

Beat egg whites until frothy. Add sugar and vanilla. Beat until stiff. Spoon over cooled filling. Sprinkle with coconut. Return to 350°F (180°C) oven to brown, about 10 minutes. Cuts into 12 generous pieces.

No wonder we don't get many home runs with a shortstop in between bases.

MINCE TARTS

These come complete with lids. A mild mincemeat flavor. Freezer handy. Recipe may be halved.

Pie crust, your own or a mix, see page 105

Mincemeat	4 cups	1 L
Apple sauce	14 oz.	398 mL
Minute tapioca	3 tbsp.	50 mL

Roll pie crust. Cut in circles to fit muffin cups. Cut smaller circles to fit top.

Stir mincemeat, (excellent if put in blender first), apple sauce and tapioca together. Fill shells. Moisten edges. Press top pastry circles around edges to seal. Cut 2 or 3 small slits in top. Sprinkle with a bit of granulated sugar. Bake on lowest shelf in 400°F (200°C) oven until browned. Serve warm with ice cream. They freeze well.

FRUIT TORTE

A simple quick dessert similar to, but different from, Fruit Cocktail Bars in Company's Coming — 150 DELICIOUS SQUARES.

All-purpose flour	1 cup	250 mL
Granulated sugar	1 cup	250 mL
Baking soda	1 tsp.	5 mL
Salt	¼ tsp.	1 mL
Egg, beaten	1	1
Fruit cocktail, drained	14 oz.	398 mL
Vanilla	1 tsp.	5 mL
Packed brown sugar	½ cup	125 mL
Chopped walnuts	½ cup	125 mL

Measure flour, sugar, baking soda and salt into mixing bowl. Stir to mix.

Add egg, fruit and vanilla. Stir until moistened. Spread into greased 8 x 8-inch (20 x 20 cm) pan.

Mix brown sugar and nuts together well. Sprinkle over top. Bake in 325°F (160°C) oven for about 45 minutes. Serve warm with cream, ice cream or Brown Sugar Sauce, page 142. Serves 9.

RAISIN PUDDING

Rich and exceptionally good. Make and bake today or make today, chill and bake tomorrow.

Butter or margarine	1 cup	250 mL
Granulated sugar	2 cups	500 mL
Egg yolks	4	4
Sherry (or fruit juice)	½ cup	125 mL
Raisins	1 cup	250 mL
Vanilla wafer crumbs, 1 box	3 cups	700 mL
Egg whites, beaten stiff	4	4
Chopped pecans (can use less)	2 cups	500 mL

Put butter and sugar in saucepan. Heat and stir over medium heat to melt butter. Cool.

Beat egg yolks and sherry. Stir into butter mixture.

Stir in raisins and wafer crumbs. Fold in egg whites and nuts. Turn into greased 9 x 13–inch (22 x 33 cm) pan. Chill overnight. The next day, bake in 400°F (200°C) oven for 20 minutes or until an inserted toothpick comes out clean. Serve warm or cold topped with whipped cream. Serves 12.

CARROT PUDDING

An old standby. Good and fruity, dark and moist.

Grated carrots	1 cup	250 mL
Grated potatoes	1 cup	250 mL
Ground suet	1 cup	250 mL
Granulated sugar	1 cup	250 mL
Raisins	1 cup	250 mL
Currants	¼ cup	50 mL
All–purpose flour	1½ cups	375 mL
Baking powder	1 tsp.	5 mL
Baking soda	1 tsp.	5 mL
Cinnamon	1 tsp.	5 mL
Allspice	½ tsp.	2 mL

Measure ingredients into large mixing bowl in order given. Stir together well. Pack into greased 10–cup (3 L) pudding pan, or use sealer jars, vegetable or juice cans or even a bowl, filling ⅔ full. Cover with foil. Secure with string. Steam for at least 3 hours. Serve with Brown Sugar Sauce, page 142. Ice cream makes a good addition. Hard Sauce, page 141, may be used instead. Serves 15.

Pictured on page 143.

CRÈME BRÛLÉE

No need to go to an expensive restaurant to enjoy this. Much easier to make than you think. So delicious with its brown sugar crust.

Egg yolks	4	4
Brown sugar	4 tbsp.	60 mL
Vanilla	1 tsp.	5 mL
Whipping cream, heat to scald	2 cups	500 mL
Brown sugar	4 tbsp.	60 mL

Beat egg yolks, first amount of brown sugar and vanilla in medium size bowl. Add hot cream slowly to egg mixture stirring continually. Return to saucepan. Cook and stir to thicken. Pour into 4 custard cups. Chill several hours.

About 2 or 3 hours before serving, cover each cup with 1 tbsp. (15 mL) sugar. Broil 6 to 8 inches (15–20 cm) from heat. Watch carefully. Let stand 15 minutes. Chill to serve cold. Before thickening, this may be poured into custard cups and baked in water-lined pan in 325°F (160°C) oven for about 30 minutes. Chill and sugar as above. Serves 4.

TRIFLE IN A PAN

Here is a way to make a moist trifle and know exactly how many servings it will provide. Simple to make and store.

White cake (½ cake mix or your own) baked in 9 × 9-inch (22 × 22 cm) pan	1	1
Sherry sprinkle (or fruit juice)		
Raspberry jam	½ cup	125 mL
Vanilla pudding and pie filling, 4 serving size	1	1
Milk	2 cups	450 mL
Envelope of topping, prepared	1	1

Sprinkle cake with sherry and let soak in. Spread with raspberry jam.

Cook pudding with milk according to directions on package. Cool thoroughly. Spread over jam layer.

Cover with topping or whipped cream. Chill until ready to use. Cuts into 9 generous pieces.

PRALINE PIE

A tasty treat. Looks good and is easy to make. The syrupy layer is hidden beneath the filling.

Butter or margarine	⅓ cup	75 mL
Brown sugar, packed	⅓ cup	75 mL
Chopped pecans	½ cup	125 mL
Baked 9-inch (22 cm) pie shell	1	1
Vanilla instant pudding, 6 serving size	1	1
Milk	2½ cups	575 mL
Whipping cream (or 1 env. topping)	1 cup	250 mL
Sugar	1 tbsp.	15 mL
Pecans, chopped or whole for topping		

Measure butter, sugar and pecans into saucepan. Heat and stir just until butter is melted and sugar is dissolved. Spread on bottom of cooked pie shell. Bake in 450°F (230°C) oven for 5 minutes to set. Cool.

Beat pudding and milk together slowly for 2 minutes.

Whip cream and sugar until stiff. Reserve ½ cup (125 mL) for garnish. Fold remaining whipped cream into pudding. Spread in pie shell. Spoon reserved whipped cream in center or in little dabs around outside edge. Garnish with pecans. Chill 3 or 4 hours. Serves 6.

Those young doctors think socialized medicine means dating their patients.

PACKAGED MILK PUDDINGS

A great way to extend a good quality pudding.

Milk	2½ cups	575 mL
Pudding powder, 4 serving size, any flavor (not instant)	1	1
Cornstarch	1 tbsp.	15 mL
Salt	½ tsp.	2 mL
Milk	½ cup	125 mL

Heat first amount of milk in heavy saucepan over medium heat until boiling.

Mix pudding powder, cornstarch and salt together in small bowl. Stir in remaining milk gradually until smooth. Pour into boiling milk stirring constantly. Cook and stir until thickened. Pour into bowl. Press waxed paper over top of hot pudding to cool without a "top" forming. Serves 6.

STEAMED GINGER PUDDING

An old recipe from away back.

All-purpose flour	2 cups	500 mL
Granulated sugar	2 tbsp.	30 mL
Ginger	1 tsp.	5 mL
Butter or margarine	¼ cup	50 mL
Raisins	½ cup	125 mL
Molasses	2 tbsp.	30 mL
Baking soda	1 tsp.	5 mL
Milk	1 cup	250 mL

Measure flour, sugar and ginger into bowl. Add butter and mix until crumbly. Stir in raisins to coat with flour mixture.

Add molasses. Stir baking soda into milk and add. Stir to mix. Pour into greased mold. Cover with foil and tie with string. Put in steamer with water ⅔ up sides of mold. Steam 2 hours. Serve with Brown Sugar Sauce, page 142. Serves 6.

BROWN BETTY

An all time favorite. Good hot or cold.

Cooking apples, peeled and sliced	6 cups	1.5 L
Granulated sugar	¾ cup	175 mL
TOPPING		
All-purpose flour	1¼ cups	300 mL
Brown sugar, packed	¾ cup	175 mL
Butter or margarine	½ cup	125 mL
Salt	½ tsp.	2 mL

Fill 10-inch (25 cm) round casserole with apples about 2-3 inches deep. Pour granulated sugar over top.

Topping: Mix flour, brown sugar, butter and salt until crumbly. Scatter over sugared apples. Pat down lightly with hand. Bake, uncovered, in 375°F (190°C) oven for about 40 minutes until apples are tender. Serve with cream or ice cream. Serves 8 generously.

RHUBARB BETTY: Use sliced fresh or frozen rhubarb, instead of apple, with a touch more sugar. Better yet, add a few raisins and omit the extra sugar. Equally as good.

FRESH FRUIT BETTY: Use fresh peaches, peeled and sliced, or fresh apricots, quartered, instead of apple.

DEEP APPLE: Sprinkle apples with cinnamon. Cover with pastry. Cut slits in top. Sprinkle with a bit of granulated sugar. Bake as above.

Paré Pointer

An experienced drinker decided to write a song about drinking but he couldn't make it past the first two bars.

BREAD PUDDING

An old time favorite.

Milk	2 cups	500 mL
Bread cubes (stale)	2 cups	500 mL
Butter or margarine	¼ cup	50 mL
Eggs, beaten	2	2
Granulated sugar	⅓ cup	75 mL
Salt	½ tsp.	2 mL
Vanilla	1 tsp.	5 mL
Raisins or currants (may use less)	1 cup	250 mL
Cinnamon or nutmeg (optional)	½ tsp.	2 mL

Measure milk into heavy saucepan. Heat until almost boiling. Add bread cubes and butter. Remove from heat.

Stir in eggs, sugar, salt, vanilla and raisins. Add cinnamon or nutmeg. Turn into 8–inch (20 cm) casserole. Bake uncovered in 350°F (180°C) oven for 45 minutes until set. Serve with cream or ice cream. Serves 6–8.

Variation: Use brown sugar instead of white. It gives it a mild but-terscotch flavor.

Variation: For a less custardy pudding, double amount of bread.

CHOCOLATE BREAD PUDDING: Mix in 2 tbsp. (30 mL) cocoa to pudding before placing in oven. Adding cinnamon is an option. Medium chocolate color and flavor. Good.

QUEEN OF PUDDINGS: Use 3 egg yolks in pudding. When baked, turn oven to 400°F (200°C). Beat 3 egg whites and ¼ tsp. (1 mL) cream of tartar until soft peaks form. Beat in 3 tbsp. (50 mL) granulated sugar until stiff. Spread on top of baked pudding. Return to oven for about 5 minutes until browned.

CHERRY COBBLER

Begin with this colorful cobbler but then be sure to try the variation. Quick and simple to prepare.

Cherry pie filling	19 oz.	540 mL
Lemon juice	1 tsp.	5 mL
Almond flavoring	½ tsp.	2 mL
All-purpose flour	1 cup	250 mL
Granulated sugar	¼ cup	50 mL
Baking powder	2 tsp.	10 mL
Salt	½ tsp.	2 mL
Cold butter or margarine	3 tbsp.	50 mL
Cold milk	½ cup	125 mL

Mix first 3 ingredients together. Spoon into 8-inch (20 cm) casserole. Place in hot oven while preparing topping.

Measure flour, sugar, baking powder and salt into bowl. Cut in butter until crumbly.

Add milk all at once. Mix to moisten. Drop by spoonfuls over hot cherry mixture. Bake uncovered in 425°F (220°C) oven for about 20-25 minutes until risen and browned.

Variation: Use any filling sweetened and thickened as if preparing for a pie filling.

Pictured on page 143.

BLUEBERRY COBBLER: Use blueberry pie filling instead of cherry.

It turned out to be dangerous to trace his family tree. He found out he was the sap.

TRIFLE

You needn't start from scratch to make this. Leftover cake works just as well. A gorgeous large bowlful.

Baked white cake, 2 layer size	1	1
Raspberry jam		
Vanilla pudding and pie filling, 6 serving size	1	1
Milk	3 cups	700 mL
Sherry or fruit juice		
Whipping cream (or 1 env. topping)	1 cup	250 mL
Granulated sugar	1 tbsp.	15 mL
Vanilla	½ tsp.	2 mL

Spread each cake layer with raspberry jam. Cut into chunks.

Cook pudding with milk according to package directions. Cool to room temperature. Hasten cooling by placing pan in cold water, stirring often.

Whip cream, sugar and vanilla until stiff. Make layers of cake chunks, a generous sprinkle of sherry and pudding in glass bowl, using as many layers as needed according to size of bowl. Make the last layer pudding. Spread whipped cream over top. Chill. Serves 16.

FRUIT TRIFLE: Drain tin of 14 oz. (398 mL) fruit cocktail and layer fruit with pudding and cake.

The waiter calls the small change left by a snob "the tip of the iceberg".

BLUEBERRY GRUNT

It is said of this old recipe that it made a grunting sound as it cooked, thus the name.

Blueberries, fresh or frozen	5 cups	1.25 L
Granulated sugar	1 cup	250 mL
Water	½ cup	125 mL
Lemon juice	1 tsp.	5 mL

TOPPING		
All-purpose flour	2 cups	500 mL
Granulated sugar	¼ cup	60 mL
Baking powder	2 tsp.	10 mL
Salt	½ tsp.	2 mL
Butter or margarine	2 tbsp.	30 mL
Milk	1 cup	250 mL

Combine blueberries, sugar, water and lemon juice in large saucepan. Heat until boiling. Simmer gently while preparing topping.

Topping: Measure flour, sugar, baking powder and salt into bowl. Stir to mix. Cut in butter.

Add milk. Mix until moistened. Drop by spoonfuls onto simmering berries. Simmer, covered, for 15 minutes without peeking. Serve warm with cream or ice cream. Serves 8.

Pictured on page 143.

A seafood diet is the best. Whenever you see food, eat it.

MINUTE TAPIOCA PUDDING

A frothy milk pudding with a butterscotch flavor. Anything but ordinary. A family favorite.

Egg yolk	1	1
Milk	2 cups	500 mL
Brown sugar, packed	⅓ cup	75 mL
Butter or margarine	¼ cup	50 mL
Minute tapioca	3 tbsp.	50 mL
Salt	⅛ tsp.	0.5 mL
Egg white	1	1
Brown sugar	2 tbsp.	30 mL
Vanilla	½ tsp.	2 mL

Put egg yolk into heavy saucepan. Stir in a small amount of milk until smooth, then stir in rest of milk followed by the next 4 ingredients. Heat and stir over medium heat until mixture comes to a full rolling boil. Remove from heat. It will seem too runny but will thicken on standing.

Beat egg white in medium bowl until soft peaks form. Add half of the brown sugar at a time continuing to beat until stiff. Add vanilla. Pour hot tapioca–milk mixture slowly into beaten egg white folding as you pour. Serve warm. Leftovers may be eaten cold. Serves 6.

REGULAR MINUTE TAPIOCA: Use granulated sugar instead of brown. A few chopped nuts may be added.

CHOCOLATE MINUTE TAPIOCA: Add 3 tbsp. (50 mL) chocolate drink powder to first ingredients.

Don't save money for a rainy day. It is a lot more fun to spend it in the sunshine.

almond flavor)
Cranraisens 5 Good!
01/31/01

03/02/99 (no D-boiler used)
nice Try again.

CREAMY RICE PUDDING

Makes a nice creamy dessert using leftover or freshly cooked rice.

Cooked rice	1½ cups	375 mL
Milk	1½ cups	375 mL
Granulated sugar	¼ cup	50 mL
Vanilla	1 tsp.	5 mL
Raisins	⅓ cup	75 mL
Butter or margarine	1 tbsp.	15 mL

Combine all 6 ingredients in top of double boiler. Cook over simmering water, stirring occasionally. When thickened, pour into serving bowl. Serve hot today and leftovers cold tomorrow. Serves 6. *Takes a while to Thicken*

CREAMY RICE CUSTARD: Add 2 slightly beaten eggs at the last. Stir continuously as it cooks until it coats a metal spoon. Serves 6.

CHOCOLATE RICE PUDDING: Add 2 tbsp. (30 mL) cocoa.

RICE MERINGUE PUDDING

A top-of-the-stove dessert, finished in the oven with a golden crown. Fast and easy.

Short grain rice	½ cup	125 mL
Milk	4 cups	1 L
Granulated sugar	½ cup	125 mL
Lemon juice	2 tsp.	10 mL
Salt	½ tsp.	2 mL
Egg yolks, fork beaten	3	3
Vanilla	1 tsp.	5 mL
Egg whites	3	3
Cream of tartar	¼ tsp.	1 mL
Granulated sugar	3 tbsp.	50 mL

Measure first 5 ingredients into large saucepan. Bring to a boil. Simmer slowly, covered, until rice is tender (about 15 minutes) stirring occasionally. Remove from heat.

Stir a bit of hot rice into egg yolks, then stir back into pot of rice. Cook to thicken. Add vanilla. Spoon into 8 inch (20 cm) casserole. Smooth top.

Beat egg whites and cream of tartar until soft peaks form. Add sugar gradually beating until stiff. Spread over top of hot rice mixture. Bake in 400°F (200°C) oven for 5 minutes or until lightly browned.

BANANA WAFER PUDDING

The wafers soften but don't disappear in this meringue crowned dessert. Good.

Granulated sugar	¾ cup	175 mL
All-purpose flour	¼ cup	50 mL
Salt	⅛ tsp.	0.5 mL
Egg yolks	3	3
Milk	2 cups	450 mL
Vanilla	1 tsp.	5 mL
Box of vanilla wafers	8 oz.	250 g
Bananas, sliced	2	2
Egg whites, room temperature	3	3
Cream of tartar	¼ tsp.	1 mL
Granulated sugar	¼ cup	50 mL

In top of double boiler, mix sugar, flour and salt. Stir in egg yolks, milk and vanilla. Cook, stirring often, until thickened and coats a metal spoon.

Layer wafers with bananas and pudding in an 8-inch (20 cm) casserole.

Beat egg whites and cream of tartar until soft peaks form. Add sugar gradually, beating until stiff. Spread over top. Bake in 400°F (200°C) oven for about 4 or 5 minutes until golden brown. Serve cold. Makes 6 servings.

LEMON CHIFFON

This has to be one of the quickest and easiest desserts going. Refreshing.

Lemon pie filling (not instant), enough for 1 pie	1	1
Egg whites, stiffly beaten	2	2

Make up lemon pudding and pie filling according to package directions using 2 egg yolks.

Fold beaten egg whites into hot pudding. Pour into serving bowl. Serve warm or cold with or without cream. Serves 6.

PLUM PUDDING

A good choice for a fruit pudding. The bread crumbs help keep it soft. Keeps for ages. Freezes well.

Ground suet	1 cup	250 mL
Granulated sugar	1 cup	250 mL
Raisins	2 cups	450 mL
Cut mixed candied fruit	1 cup	250 mL
Cut up dates	¾ cup	175 mL
Cut mixed peel	½ cup	125 mL
All-purpose flour	1¼ cups	300 mL
Dry bread crumbs	1¼ cups	300 mL
Baking powder	2 tsp.	10 mL
Salt	1¼ tsp.	6 mL
Cinnamon	1 tsp.	5 mL
Nutmeg	1 tsp.	5 mL
Baking soda	½ tsp.	2 mL
Eggs	2	2
Milk	¾ cup	175 mL

Measure first 6 ingredients into large mixing bowl. Mix well.

Add next 7 ingredients. Stir together to mix.

In small bowl, beat eggs until frothy. Mix in milk. Pour into suet-flour mixture. Stir together until evenly moistened. Pack into greased 2-quart (2.5 L) pudding pan. Cover with foil and secure with string. Place on rack in large pot. Pour boiling water half way up pudding pan. Cover and boil. Steam 3 hours, adding boiling water as needed. Serve with Brown Sugar Sauce, page 142. Serves 12 to 15.

To keep soldiers gambling poor, they are confined to quarters.

SPANISH CREAM

This old recipe fills the bill for a light touch after a heavy meal. A white dessert to show off a sauce of your choice.

Milk	3 cups	700 mL
Unflavored gelatin powder	¼ oz.	7 g
Granulated sugar	½ cup	125 mL
Salt	¼ tsp.	1 mL
Egg yolks	3	3
Vanilla	1 tsp.	5 mL
Egg whites	3	3

Measure milk into top of double boiler. Sprinkle gelatin over top. Let stand for 5 minutes, then heat over simmering water.

Add sugar and salt. Mix a little of the hot mixture into egg yolks, then pour yolks and vanilla into double boiler. Cook and stir until mixture coats a metal spoon. This will take close to 15 minutes. Remove from heat. Chill until it thickens enough to pile softly when spooned from one side to the other.

Beat egg whites until stiff. Fold into thickened mixture. Pour into pretty bowl or mold. Chill. Serve with whipped cream, Deluxe Chocolate Sauce, page 139, or Butterscotch Sauce, page 139, Melba Sauce, page 136, is very pretty. Serves 8.

CHOCLATE SPANISH CREAM: Add 1½ squares of unsweetened chocolate to milk in double boiler.

1. Melba Puffs page 103.
2. Apple Dumplings page 99.
3. After Dinner Mints page 145.
4. Blueberry Crêpes page 104.
5. Blueberry Sauce page 136.

QUICK APPLE PUDDING

Aroma and flavor go hand in hand. Scrumptious.

Apples, peeled and sliced	3 cups	700 mL
Granulated sugar	½ cup	125 mL
Cinnamon sprinkle		
Butter or margarine, softened	¼ cup	50 mL
Granulated sugar	½ cup	125 mL
Egg, beaten	1	1
Milk	½ cup	125 mL
Vanilla	½ tsp.	2 mL
All-purpose flour	1 cup	250 mL
Baking powder	2 tsp.	10 mL
Salt	¼ tsp.	1 mL
Brown sugar, packed	1 cup	250 mL
All-purpose flour	3 tbsp.	50 mL
Butter or margarine	1 tbsp.	15 mL
Vanilla	1 tsp.	5 mL
Hot water	1½ cup	375 mL

Place apples and sugar into 3 quart (3 L) casserole. Toss together. Sprinkle with cinnamon.

Measure next 8 ingredients into bowl. Mix well. Spoon over apples.

Mix brown sugar and flour thoroughly in bowl. Stir in butter, vanilla and water. Pour over batter. Do not stir. Bake, uncovered, in 350°F (180°C) oven for 45 minutes or until apples are baked and pudding is firm to touch. Serves 8.

He who laughs last probably didn't get the joke.

SAUCY FUDGE PUDDING

The fudge batter rises to the top as it bakes, leaving a rich chocolate sauce beneath.

All-purpose flour	1 cup	250 mL
Granulated sugar	¾ cup	175 mL
Cocoa	2 tbsp.	30 mL
Baking powder	2 tsp.	10 mL
Salt	¼ tsp.	1 mL
Milk	½ cup	125 mL
Cooking oil (or butter, melted)	2 tbsp.	30 mL
Chopped nuts, optional	½ cup	125 mL
Packed brown sugar	¾ cup	175 mL
Cocoa	2 tbsp.	30 mL
Hot water	1¾ cup	425 mL

Measure flour, sugar, cocoa, baking powder and salt into bowl. Stir. Add milk, oil and nuts, if you are using them. Mix together with spoon and scrape into 8-inch (20 cm) casserole or pan.

In same bowl mix sugar and cocoa together. Add water. Stir to dissolve sugar. Pour over batter but do not stir. Bake, uncovered, in 350°F (180°C) oven for about 40 minutes until batter has risen above sauce and is firm to touch. Serves 6.

STRAWBERRY BUTTERSCOTCH

An unlikely combination. A pretty dishful. A light, tasty dessert.

Butterscotch or caramel pudding and pie filling, 6 serving size, cooked as package directs	1	1
Canned or frozen strawberries, with juice	1 cup	250 mL
Whipping cream (or 1 env. topping)	1 cup	250 mL
Granulated sugar	1 tbsp.	15 mL
Vanilla	½ tsp.	2 mL

Spoon cooked and chilled pudding into 6 sherbets or fruit nappies. Spoon strawberries over top.

Whip cream, sugar and vanilla until stiff. Put a dollop on top of each. Serves 6.

LEMON SAUCED PUDDING

As the batter cooks, it rises to the top. Makes a light pudding with lemon sauce to spoon over top.

Egg whites	2	2
Butter or margarine, softened	1 tbsp.	15 mL
Granulated sugar	1 cup	225 mL
All-purpose flour	¼ cup	50 mL
Egg yolks	2	2
Lemon, juice and grated rind	1	1
Salt	⅛ tsp.	0.5 mL
Milk	1½ cups	350 mL

Beat egg whites in small bowl until stiff. Set aside.

Measure butter, sugar, flour, egg yolks, lemon juice, rind, salt and milk into mixing bowl. Beat lightly until blended. Fold in beaten egg whites. Turn into 8-inch (20 cm) casserole. Set in pan of hot water and bake in 350°F (180°C) oven for about 45 minutes until browned. Makes 6 servings.

Riding a horse bareback really makes you feel better off.

ENGLISH TRIFLE

This has a homemade custard but a vanilla pudding mix may be substituted. Very moist.

White cake, your own or a mix	1	1
Whole frozen strawberries, thawed and sliced	2 cups	500 mL
Granulated sugar	¼ cup	50 mL
Sherry (or fruit juice with 2 tsp. 10 mL, brandy flavoring)	½ cup	125 mL
Custard powder	3 tbsp.	50 mL
Granulated sugar	3 tbsp.	50 mL
Milk	2 cups	450 mL
Vanilla	½ tsp.	2 mL
Whipping cream (or 1 env. topping)	1 cup	250 mL
Granulated sugar	1 tbsp.	15 mL
Vanilla	½ tsp.	2 mL
Cherries for garnish		

Crumble cake with your hands into large bowl.

In another bowl, combine and stir berries, sugar and sherry. Empty into cake crumbs. Stir together.

Put custard powder and sugar into saucepan. Gradually mix in milk and vanilla. Cook and stir over medium heat until it boils and thickens. Remove from heat. Cool. Pour over cake mixture. Stir to distribute evenly.

Whip cream, sugar and vanilla until stiff. Smooth over top. Garnish with cherries. Chill. Serves 15.

STEAMED VANILLA PUDDING

A flavor everyone is sure to enjoy.

Butter or margarine	¼ cup	60 mL
Granulated sugar, softened	½ cup	125 mL
Egg, beaten	1	1
Vanilla	1 tsp.	5 mL
Raisins or currants	1 cup	250 mL
All-purpose flour	1½ cups	350 mL
Baking powder	1 tbsp.	15 mL
Salt	½ tsp.	2 mL
Milk	⅔ cup	150 mL

Cream butter and sugar together well. Add beaten egg and vanilla. Beat well. Stir in raisins.

Mix flour, baking powder and salt together. Add alternately with milk, stirring after each addition.

Grease and sugar a 4-cup (1 L) mold. Spoon in batter. Cover with foil, securing with string. Steam, with water halfway up side of mold, for about 1½ hours. Test with wooden pick. Serve with Brown Sugar Sauce, page 142. Serves 6.

CRANBERRY PUDDING: Add 1 cup coarsely chopped cranberries plus ¼ cup (50 mL) more sugar to creamed mixture.

BANANA CREAM PUDDING

A quick dessert which can make use of those ripe bananas.

Milk	2 cups	500 mL
Granulated sugar	½ cup	125 mL
All-purpose flour	2 tbsp.	30 mL
Salt	¼ tsp.	1 mL
Egg	1	1
Bananas, sliced	2	2
Vanilla	½ tsp.	2 mL

Heat milk in top of double boiler over boiling water.

In small bowl, stir sugar, flour, salt and egg. Pour into hot milk stirring until thickened and mixture coats metal spoon. Remove from heat. Cool, stirring occasionally.

When cool, stir in bananas and vanilla. Serves 6-8.

SAUCED BUTTERSCOTCH

Pudding and a yummy sauce cooked in the same dish.

All-purpose flour	1 cup	250 mL
Granulated sugar	½ cup	125 mL
Baking powder	2 tsp.	10 mL
Salt	⅛ tsp.	0.5 mL
Milk	½ cup	125 mL
Butter or margarine, softened	2 tbsp.	30 mL
Raisins	½ cup	125 mL
Packed brown sugar	1 cup	250 mL
Butter or margarine	1 tbsp.	15 mL
Vanilla	1 tsp.	5 mL
Hot water	2 cups	500 mL

Measure first 7 ingredients into bowl. Mix together with spoon. Turn into greased 8-inch (20 cm) casserole or pan.

In same bowl stir sugar, butter, vanilla and hot water until sugar dissolves. Pour over batter. Do not stir. Bake in 350°F (180°C) oven for about 30 minutes until sauce is on the bottom and top crust is firm to touch. Serves 6.

QUICK PUDDING: Another family favorite. Add ½ tsp. (3 mL) cinnamon to sauce before pouring over batter.

MOCHA SAUCED PUDDING: Omit last 4 ingredients for sauce. Mix together 2 tbsp. (30 mL) cocoa and 1 cup (250 mL) brown sugar. Stir 2 tsp. (10 mL) instant coffee into 2 cups (500 mL) hot water. Add to cocoa-sugar mixture. Pour over batter.

CRÈME CARAMEL

Usually associated with top-notch restaurants, this delicious custard, sauced in caramel, is much easier to make than you think. Only the explanation is lengthy.

Granulated sugar	1 cup	250 mL
Water	½ cup	125 mL
CUSTARD		
Eggs	3	3
Milk	2 cups	500 mL
Granulated sugar	¼ cup	50 mL
Salt	¼ tsp.	1 mL
Vanilla	1 tsp.	5 mL

Heat first amount of sugar in heavy pan over medium heat. Stir as sugar melts until completely melted and it turns a rich caramel color. If too light, it has no flavor, if too dark it will be bitter. Add water carefully. It will sputter with a vengeance. Stir until blended well. It will thicken as it blends. Pour into bottom of 6 custard cups, ring pan or casserole. Tilt cups (or container) to distribute caramelized sugar over bottom and part way up sides to coat well.

Custard: Beat eggs lightly in mixing bowl. Add milk, sugar, salt and vanilla. Beat together slightly. Pour into custard cups. Set cups in pan with ½ inch (1.5 cm) hot water in it. Bake in 325°F (160°C) oven for about 35 minutes until a knife inserted near outside edge comes out clean. Allow to cool ½ hour at room temperature. Chill for at least 3 hours. To unmold, run knife around edge. Dip bottom in hot water for a few moments. Place small plate over top and invert together. Remove cup. Serve to 6 lucky people.

Pictured on page 143.

CUSTARD: Omit first step of burning sugar and adding water. Mix custard, pour into 6½-inch (16 cm) casserole. Sprinkle with nutmeg. Place in pan of water. Bake in 325°F (160°C) oven for about 1 hour until a knife, inserted half way between center and edge, comes out clean. Serve cold. Serves 4-6.

CUSTARD SAUCE: Pour beaten custard ingredients into top of double boiler. Omit nutmeg. Cook and stir over gently boiling water until mixture coats a metal spoon. Serve over fruit, pie, cake or ice cream.

CHOCOLATE CUSTARD: Add 2 tbsp. (30 mL) cocoa to Custard Sauce. Double amount of sugar.

BLUEBERRY BUCKLE

Good flavor as well as good looks.

Butter or margarine, softened	¼ cup	60 mL
Granulated sugar	½ cup	125 mL
Egg	1	1
All-purpose flour	1 cup	250 mL
Baking powder	1½ tsp.	7 mL
Salt	¼ tsp.	1 mL
Milk	⅓ cup	75 mL
Blueberries, fresh or frozen	2 cups	500 mL
TOPPING		
Granulated sugar	⅓ cup	75 mL
All-purpose flour	⅓ cup	75 mL
Butter or margarine	¼ cup	50 mL
Cinnamon	½ tsp.	2 mL

Cream butter and sugar well. Beat in egg.

Stir in flour, baking powder and salt.

Add milk and mix. Spread in greased 8 × 8-inch (20 × 20 cm) pan.

Spread blueberries over top.

Topping: Mix all 4 ingredients together until crumbly. Scatter over blueberries. Bake in 350°F (180°C) oven for 40-50 minutes until done. It should show signs of pulling away from edge of pan. Serves 9.

She couldn't care less for a man's company. Unless he owns it, that is.

BLANC MANGE

As the name implies, it is white food. Similar to a custard but uses no eggs for thickening.

Milk	1¾ cups	400 mL
Granulated sugar	½ cup	125 mL
Cornstarch	4 tbsp.	60 mL
Salt	⅛ tsp.	0.5 mL
Milk	¼ cup	50 mL
Vanilla	½ tsp.	2 mL

Combine first amount of milk with sugar in heavy saucepan. Slowly bring to a boil.

Mix cornstarch, salt and second amount of milk together. Stir into boiling milk. Simmer and stir for 5 minutes. Remove from heat.

Stir in vanilla. Pour into bowl. Chill. Serve with fresh or canned fruit.

Note: Custard powder may be used instead of cornstarch and vanilla.

CHOCOLATE BLANC MANGE: After removing from heat, stir in ½ cup (125 mL) semisweet chocolate chips until melted. Chill.

BUTTERSCOTCH BLANC MANGE: Use brown sugar, packed, instead of white.

When college students were advised they were to have a blood test the next day, they stayed up half the night studying for it.

BLUEBERRY SAUCE

If you want a filling from scratch, this is an excellent way to get that good fresh taste.

Blueberries, fresh or frozen	10 oz.	284 g
Water	½ cup	125 mL
Granulated sugar	½ cup	125 mL
Cornstarch	1 tbsp.	15 mL
Lemon juice	1 tbsp.	15 mL

Combine all ingredients together in saucepan. Stir well. Heat and stir over medium heat until boiling. Simmer gently for about 5 minutes until berries release their juice. Good over crêpes and waffles.

Pictured on page 125.

MELBA SAUCE

A gorgeous red. Livens up many desserts.

Frozen raspberries, thawed and drained, juice reserved	15 oz.	425 mL
Raspberry juice plus water to make	1¼ cups	300 mL
Cornstarch	4 tsp.	20 mL
Granulated sugar	2 tbsp.	30 mL

Combine raspberry juice, cornstarch and sugar in saucepan. Heat and stir over medium heat until it boils and thickens. Add raspberries. Blend in blender and strain or force through sieve to remove seeds. Cool. Serve over Peach Melba, page 87, Blanc Mange, page 135, Custard, page 133, Melba Puffs, page 103, etc.

Pictured on page 125.

SWEETENED CONDENSED MILK

Make your own for both economy and convenience.

Powdered skim milk	1 cup	250 mL
Granulated sugar	2/3 cup	150 mL
Water	1/3 cup	75 mL
Butter or margarine	1/4 cup	60 mL

Measure all ingredients into blender. Blend until smooth. Use as any sweetened condensed milk. Makes equivalent of 1 can.

FRUIT TOPPING

Just right to top off any fruit dessert or use as a fruit dip. So easy. So good.

Whipping cream (or 1 env. topping)	1 cup	250 mL
Raspberry flavored yogurt	1 cup	250 mL

Beat cream until stiff. Mix in yogurt. Serve as a topping for fruit or as a dip. Makes 3 cups (700 mL).

PINEAPPLE SAUCE

For a thicker, more fruity sauce, simply omit extra pineapple juice.

Crushed pineapple with juice	14 oz.	398 mL
Pineapple juice	1 cup	250 mL
Granulated sugar	1/3 cup	75 mL
Cornstarch	4 tsp.	20 mL

Mix all together in saucepan. Heat and stir until boiled and thickened. Makes 2 3/4 cups (650 mL).

ORANGE SAUCE

Soft and fluffy. Pile on a slice of angel food or chocolate cake or a crêpe or into a chocolate cup. Even on cheesecake. So versatile.

Egg yolk	1	1
Frozen orange juice, concentrated, thawed	½ cup	125 mL
Water	1 cup	250 mL
Grated orange rind	1 tsp.	5 mL
Lemon juice	2 tsp.	10 mL
Butter or margarine	1 tbsp.	15 mL
Granulated sugar	⅔ cup	150 mL
All-purpose flour	2 tbsp.	30 mL
Salt	¼ tsp.	1 mL
Water	¼ cup	50 mL
Egg white	1	1
Whipping cream	1 cup	250 mL

Beat egg yolk with a spoon in heavy saucepan. Add orange juice gradually. Stir in first amount of water, rind, lemon juice and butter. Heat over medium heat until boiling.

Stir sugar, flour and salt together. Mix in second amount of water. Pour into orange mixture, stirring until it boils and thickens. Cool.

Beat egg white until stiff. Using same beaters, beat cream until stiff. Fold egg white into cooled mixture then fold in whipped cream. Serve over puddings, angel food cake, fruit or ice cream. Makes 3½ cups (800 mL).

SIMPLE ORANGE SAUCE

A good make-ahead that stores well.

Orange juice	1 cup	250 mL
Cornstarch	2 tbsp.	30 mL
Granulated sugar	¾ cup	175 mL
Grated orange rind	1 tsp.	5 mL

Mix all together in saucepan. Heat and stir over medium heat until it boils and thickens. Makes 1¼ cups (250 mL).

BUTTERSCOTCH SAUCE

An easy make-your-own sauce.

Light cream	1 cup	250 mL
Brown sugar, packed	1 cup	250 mL
Corn syrup, light or dark	1 cup	250 mL
Butter or margarine	1/3 cup	75 mL
Vanilla	1 tsp.	5 mL
Salt	1/8 tsp.	0.5 mL

Measure all ingredients into saucepan. Heat and stir over medium heat until mixture boils. Boil and stir for 2 minutes. Cool. Makes 2½ cups (575 mL).

DELUXE CHOCOLATE SAUCE

This delicious sauce keeps for ages. A real treat to have on hand.

Semisweet chocolate chips	2 cups	500 mL
Butter or margarine	1/2 cup	125 mL
Instant coffee powder	1 tbsp.	15 mL
Salt	1/8 tsp.	0.5 mL
Vanilla	1 tbsp.	15 mL
Icing (confectioner's) sugar	2 cups	500 mL
Light corn syrup	1 cup	250 mL
Hot water	1 cup	250 mL

Measure first 5 ingredients into saucepan. Heat and stir over medium heat until smooth. Remove from heat.

Beat in icing sugar, syrup and water until smooth. Pour into jar. Store in refrigerator. Makes 4½ cups (1.1 L). Serve over ice cream.

APRICOT SAUCE

A good combination of flavors. Tangy.

Apricot jam	1 cup	250 mL
Orange juice	2 tbsp.	30 mL
Brandy flavoring	1/2 tsp.	2 mL

Mix all together. Serve hot or cold over crêpes, ice cream, cake or whatever. Makes 1 cup (250 mL).

CHOCO PEANUT BUTTER TOPPING

Rich chocolate flavored enhanced peanut butter. Great for sundaes. Served hot, it thickens over ice cream.

Semisweet chocolate chips	1 cup	250 mL
Smooth peanut butter	½ cup	125 mL
Evaporated milk	⅓ cup	75 mL
Corn syrup	¼ cup	60 mL

Ice cream
Chopped walnuts or peanuts

Combine first 4 ingredients together in saucepan. Heat and stir until melted.

Scoop ice cream into dishes. Spoon hot sauce over top. Sprinkle with nuts. Makes 1 cup (250 mL).

Note: Always serve this sauce hot. It gets very thick when cold.

CHOCOLATE FONDUE

An informal way to serve dessert.

Good quality chocolate bars (Toblerone is best)	3 – 3 oz.	3 – 85 g
Heavy cream (or light will do)	½ cup	125 mL
Orange flavored liqueur (or juice)	2 tbsp.	30 mL

Break up chocolate and stir with cream and liqueur over low heat until melted. Transfer to fondue pot. Dip cake cubes, strawberries, bananas and other fresh fruit. Try Rice Krispies (150 Delicious Squares) cut into small cubes and angel food cake, cubed. Thin with cream if sauce thickens.

Variation: Use 1½ cups (375 mL) semisweet chocolate chips instead of chocolate bars.

WHITE FONDUE: Use white almond bark instead of chocolate.

FONDUE DIPPERS: Strawberries, pears, tiny puffs filled with different colors of ice cream, seedless grapes, bananas, orange sections, apple wedges, pineapple chunks, maraschino cherries, angel cake cubes, cake cubes, marshmallows, pound cake cubes, doughnut cubes, Rice Krispie Squares, cut into small cubes.

LEMON SAUCE

The perfect complement to Lemon Cheesecake or for serving over warm gingerbread.

Granulated sugar	½ cup	125 mL
Water	1 cup	250 mL
Lemon juice	3 tbsp.	50 mL
Grated lemon rind	1 tsp.	5 mL
Butter or margarine	1 tbsp.	15 mL
Salt	⅛ tsp.	0.5 mL
Water	¼ cup	50 mL
Cornstarch	4 tsp.	20 mL

Combine first 6 ingredients in saucepan. Stir and heat to boiling.

Mix water with cornstarch. Stir into hot mixture. Cook and stir until thickened. Cool. Spoon over cheesecake, cottage pudding or gingerbread.

LEMON FONDUE: Double recipe except for second amount of water and cornstarch. Multiply those 2 amounts by 4. Serve with fresh fruit, cake cubes, marshmallows and gingerbread cubes.

LEMON CREAM SAUCE: Decrease first amount of water by ½. Beat 1 cup (250 mL) whipping cream until stiff. Fold into cooled sauce.

HARD SAUCE

Rich and creamy. Serve on steamed fruit puddings and gingerbread.

Butter or margarine, softened	½ cup	125 mL
Icing (confectioner's) sugar	1 cup	250 mL
Vanilla	1 tsp.	5 mL

Beat all together. Chill in covered container. Serve on hot steamed puddings. Makes 1 cup (225 mL).

Variation: Brown sugar may be used instead of icing sugar.

RUM OR BRANDY HARD SAUCE: Add ½ tsp. (2 mL) rum or brandy flavoring. Add more to taste.

BROWN SUGAR SAUCE

The finishing touch for cottage pudding and all steamed fruit puddings.

Brown sugar, packed	1 cup	250 mL
All-purpose flour	¼ cup	50 mL
Salt	½ tsp.	2 mL
Water	2 cups	450 mL
Vanilla	1 tsp.	5 mL

Mix sugar, flour and salt together well in medium sized saucepan. This enables water to be mixed in with no lumps.

Stir in water and vanilla. Heat, stirring, over medium heat until it boils and thickens. Makes about 2½ cups (500 mL). Serve over steamed and cottage puddings.

RUM SAUCE: Add 1 tsp. (5 mL) rum flavoring. Great for Plum Pudding, page 123, and Carrot Pudding, page 111. Dark brown sugar is best for this.

Pictured on page 143.

RUM RAISIN SAUCE: Add 1 tsp. (5 mL) rum flavoring, ½ cup (125 mL) raisins and 2 tsp. (10 mL) grated lemon rind. Adding ½ cup (125 mL) chopped pecans is extra special. Serve over steamed puddings, Cottage Pudding, page 28, or ice cream.

CHOCOLATE PUDDING SAUCE: Mix in 1½ tbsp. (25 mL) cocoa with sugar mixture. Serve over chocolate cake.

VANILLA PUDDING SAUCE: Use granulated sugar instead of brown.

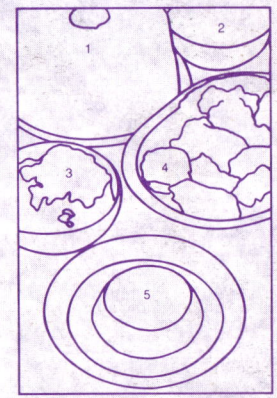

1. Carrot Pudding page 111.
2. Rum Sauce page 142.
3. Blueberry Grunt page 119.
4. Cherry Cobbler page 117.
5. Crème Caramel page 133.

AFTER DINNER MINTS

What could make a better ending than your own soft delicately-flavored, delicately-colored mints?

Icing (confectioner's) sugar	2½ cups	600 mL
Butter or margarine, softened	3 tbsp.	50 mL
Cream	2 tbsp.	30 mL
Peppermint flavoring	½ tsp.	2 mL
Food coloring		

Mix all ingredients together well. Dough should be fairly stiff but still pliable enough to roll. Add a bit more icing sugar or cream as needed for right consistency. Divide into separate chunks to tint different colors. Leave 1 chunk plain. Roll into rope about ½ inch (1.5 cm) in diameter. Cut into pieces. Let stand on waxed paper several hours, at least overnight. Makes several dozen mints. May also be pressed into candy molds.

Pictured on page 125.

CHOCOLATE COATED MINTS

Semisweet chocolate square	1	1
Butter or margarine	1 tsp.	5 mL
Coconut		

Melt over hot water. Stir until smooth. Remove from heat but return when chocolate cools. Cut ropes into 1½ inch (4 cm) lengths, dip, roll in coconut. Place on waxed paper to cool. A most impressive after-dinner treat.

PECAN BITES

Crispy little munchies.

Egg white	1	1
Brown sugar, packed	1 cup	250 mL
Vanilla	1 tsp.	5 mL
Whole pecans	2 cups	500 mL

Beat egg white until soft peaks form. Add brown sugar and beat until stiff. Mix in vanilla. Fold in nuts. Drop by teaspoon on greased baking pan. Bake in 300°F (150°C) oven for 20 minutes.

Pictured on page 89.

CHOCOLATE CHERRIES

You will get rave reviews when you serve these with coffee. Chocolate covers a peanut butter coating.

Maraschino cherries with stems, drained overnight	40 – 50	40 – 50
Smooth peanut butter	1 cup	250 mL
Icing (confectioner's) sugar	1 cup	250 mL
Butter or margarine, softened	2 tbsp.	30 mL
Semisweet chocolate squares	8	8
Grated parowax (paraffin)	¾ cup	175 mL

Have cherries very well drained and dry on paper towels overnight.

Mix peanut butter, icing sugar and butter together well. Cover each cherry with a thin coat. If it is too thick, chocolate won't cling very well.

Melt chocolate and paraffin in pan over hot water. Dip cherries into warm mixture. If chocolate is too hot it won't cling to covered cherry. Place on waxed paper. Store in covered container. These keep for weeks. Makes 40 to 50.

Note: Semisweet chocolate chips may be used — 1⅓ cups (300 mL).

TRUFFLES

This after-dinner treat melts in your mouth.

Cocoa	½ cup	125 mL
Butter or margarine, softened	½ cup	125 mL
Icing (confectioner's) sugar	1½ cups	375 mL
Chocolate sprinkle, crushed almonds, icing sugar, cocoa		

Mix cocoa, butter and icing sugar together well. Shape into balls.

Roll balls in chocolate, ground almonds, icing sugar or cocoa. Makes 16 to 24, depending on size. Chill.

CHOCOLATE CUPS

Make larger size for dessert and tiny size to hold liqueurs.

Semisweet chocolate chips or squares
Baking cups, foil or paper

Melt chips over hot water. Brush a thin layer over the inside of a baking cup. Chill until firm. Brush with another thin layer. Chill until needed. Slowly and carefully, remove paper. Fill with Orange Chantilly, Mint Chantilly or small scoop of ice cream. Several variations follow.

CHANTILLY: Impossible to pick a favorite without trying all of them. To 1 cup (250 mL) whipping cream add —

ALMOND: 1 tbsp. (15 mL) granulated sugar, ¼ tsp. (1 mL) almond flavoring.

BRANDY: MAPLE: MINT: RUM: VANILLA: 1 tbsp. (15 mL) granulated sugar, ½ tsp. (2 mL) flavoring.

BERRY: 2 tbsp. (30 mL) granulated sugar (or to taste), ½ tsp. (2 mL) vanilla, 1 cup (250 mL) sliced fresh fruit.

BUTTERSCOTCH: 2 tbsp. (30 mL) brown sugar or more, ½ tsp. (1 mL) vanilla.

CHOCOLATE: ¼ cup (60 mL) chocolate drink powder.

COFFEE: 1 tbsp. (15 mL) granulated sugar, ½ tsp. (2 mL) vanilla, 1 tsp. (5 mL) instant coffee granules, crushed.

COINTREAU: 4 tsp. (20 mL) granulated sugar, 2 tbsp. (30 mL) cointreau, or other orange liqueur.

CRÈME DE MENTHE: 2 tbsp. (30 mL) granulated sugar, 2 tbsp. (30 mL) crème de menthe.

KAHLUA: 2 tbsp. (30 mL) kahlua.

ORANGE: 1 tbsp. (15 mL) frozen concentrated orange juice.

Whip sugar and flavoring and any additions, except fresh fruit, with cream until thick. Fruit should be folded in last. Toasted, slivered almonds may be added, about ¼ cup (50 mL).

CHOCOLATE MINTS

Make your own to surprise your friends. Excellent.

Semisweet chocolate chips	1 cup	250 mL
Butter or margarine	1 tsp.	5 mL
Peppermint flavoring	½ tsp.	2 mL

Melt all together in heavy saucepan over low heat, stirring. Drop small dabs on waxed paper. Allow to set. Makes about 5 dozen.

MONTE CRISTO

A special coffee to top off a great meal.

Kahlua	1 oz.	30 mL
Grand Marnier	½ oz.	15 mL
Hot coffee		
Whipped cream		

First prepare the glasses. Moisten rim of glass with lemon juice. Dip in granulated sugar.

Pour Kahlua and Grand Marnier into glass. Add coffee to ½ inch (1 cm) from top. Add whipped cream right to the top. Do not stir. May be garnished with grated chocolate. May also drizzle a bit of Bailey's Irish Cream over whipped cream. Serves 1.

If you shout around trees you will have a petrified forest.

BLUEBERRY TEA

A special tea to follow a special meal.

Amaretto	1 oz.	30 mL
Grand Marnier	½ oz.	15 mL
Blueberry tea (or black currant or orange pekoe if necessary)		

Pour Amaretto and Grand Marnier into large brandy snifter glass. Add hot tea to taste, about ½ cup (125 mL). Serves 1.

IRISH COFFEE

A toast to the Irish.

Irish whiskey	1½ oz.	45 mL
Granulated sugar (or more — optional)	½ tsp.	2 mL
Hot coffee		
Whipped cream		

Put whiskey into Irish coffee glass. Add sugar. Fill with hot coffee to about ½ inch (1 cm) from rim. Stir. Fill to brim with whipped cream. Do not stir. Serves 1.

Pictured on page 71.

SPANISH COFFEE

Serve with greetings of Olé!

Kahlua or Tia Maria	1 oz.	30 mL
Brandy	½ oz.	15 mL
Hot coffee		
Sweetened whipped cream		

To sugar rims of glasses, dip lemon moistened rims into granulated sugar.

Put kahlua and brandy into coffee glass. Fill with coffee to within ½ inch (1 cm) from rim. Top with whipped cream to the brim. Do not stir. Serves 1.

MEASUREMENT TABLES

Throughout this book measurements are given in Conventional and Metric measure. To compensate for differences between the two measurements due to rounding, a full metric measure is not always used. The cup used is the standard 8 fluid ounce. Temperature is given in degrees Fahrenheit and Celsius. Baking pan measurements are in inches and centimetres as well as quarts and litres. An exact metric conversion is given below as well as the working equivalent (Standard Measure).

OVEN TEMPERATURES

Fahrenheit (°F)	Celsius (°C)
175°	80°
200°	95°
225°	110°
250°	120°
275°	140°
300°	150°
325°	160°
350°	175°
375°	190°
400°	205°
425°	220°
450°	230°
475°	240°
500°	260°

SPOONS

Conventional Measure	Metric Exact Conversion Millilitre (mL)	Metric Standard Measure Millilitre (mL)
1/8 teaspoon (tsp.)	0.6 mL	0.5 mL
1/4 teaspoon (tsp.)	1.2 mL	1 mL
1/2 teaspoon (tsp.)	2.4 mL	2 mL
1 teaspoon (tsp.)	4.7 mL	5 mL
2 teaspoons (tsp.)	9.4 mL	10 mL
1 tablespoon (tbsp.)	14.2 mL	15 mL

CUPS

1/4 cup (4 tbsp.)	56.8 mL	50 mL
1/3 cup (5 1/3 tbsp.)	75.6 mL	75 mL
1/2 cup (8 tbsp.)	113.7 mL	125 mL
2/3 cup (10 2/3 tbsp.)	151.2 mL	150 mL
3/4 cup (12 tbsp.)	170.5 mL	175 mL
1 cup (16 tbsp.)	227.3 mL	250 mL
4 1/2 cups	1022.9 mL	1000 mL (1 L)

PANS

Conventional Inches	Metric Centimetres
8x8 inch	20x20 cm
9x9 inch	22x22 cm
9x13 inch	22x33 cm
10x15 inch	25x38 cm
11x17 inch	28x43 cm
8x2 inch round	20x5 cm
9x2 inch round	22x5 cm
10x4 1/2 inch tube	25x11 cm
8x4x3 inch loaf	20x10x7 cm
9x5x3 inch loaf	22x12x7 cm

DRY MEASUREMENTS

Conventional Measure Ounces (oz.)	Metric Exact Conversion Grams (g)	Metric Standard Measure Grams (g)
1 oz.	28.3 g	30 g
2 oz.	56.7 g	55 g
3 oz.	85.0 g	85 g
4 oz.	113.4 g	125 g
5 oz.	141.7 g	140 g
6 oz.	170.1 g	170 g
7 oz.	198.4 g	200 g
8 oz.	226.8 g	250 g
16 oz.	453.6 g	500 g
32 oz.	907.2 g	1000 g (1 kg)

CASSEROLES (Canada & Britain)

Standard Size Casserole	Exact Metric Measure
1 qt. (5 cups)	1.13 L
1 1/2 qts. (7 1/2 cups)	1.69 L
2 qts. (10 cups)	2.25 L
2 1/2 qts. (12 1/2 cups)	2.81 L
3 qts. (15 cups)	3.38 L
4 qts. (20 cups)	4.5 L
5 qts. (25 cups)	5.63 L

CASSEROLES (United States)

Standard Size Casserole	Exact Metric Measure
1 qt. (4 cups)	900 mL
1 1/2 qts. (6 cups)	1.35 L
2 qts. (8 cups)	1.8 L
2 1/2 qts. (10 cups)	2.25 L
3 qts. (12 cups)	2.7 L
4 qts. (16 cups)	3.6 L
5 qts. (20 cups)	4.5 L

INDEX

After Dinner Mints 145
Almond Chantilly 147
An Angel's Cake 9
Angel Food Cake 19
Apple Alaska Bake 73
Apple Betty, See Brown Betty . . 115
Apple Crisp, See Brown Betty . . 115
Apple, Danish Bars 100
Apple Dumplings 99
Apple Jack 28
Apple Jelly Glaze 96
Apple Oat Squares 99
Apple Pan Dowdy 101
Apple, Quick Pudding 127
Apple, Baked 83
Apples, Baked Mincemeat 83
Apples, Fruit Compote 84
Apricot Crêpes 104
Apricot Glaze 82
Apricot Sauce 139

Baked Alaska 75
Baked Apples 83
Baked Mincemeat Apples 83
Banana Butterscotch 81
Banana, Cherry Slice 45
Banana Cream Pudding 131
Banana Split Dessert 46
Banana Wafer Pudding 122
Bananas, Sauced 91
Bavarian, Maple 52
Bavarian, Strawberry 44
Berry Chantilly 147
Berry Torte 106
Best Chocolate Cheesecake . . . 32
Beverages
   Blueberry Tea 149
   Irish Coffee 149
   Monte Cristo 148
   Spanish Coffee 149
Biscuit Shortcake 11
Black Forest Bowl 10
Black Forest Cake 10
Black Forest Crêpes 98
Black Forest, Quick 23
Black Forest Soufflé 50
Blanc Mange 135
Blitz Torte 21
Blueberry Buckle 134
Blueberry Cheesecake 30
Blueberry Cobbler 117
Blueberry Crêpes 104
Blueberry Grunt 119
Blueberry Sauce 136

Blueberry Tea 149
Bocconne Dolce 97
Boston Cream Pie 26
Brandied Peaches 88
Brandy Chantilly 147
Brandy Hard Sauce 141
Bread Pudding 116
Broken Glass 58
Brown Betty 115
Brown Sugar Sauce 142
Butterscotch Blanc Mange 135
Butterscotch Chantilly 147
Butterscotch Crêpes 104
Butterscotch Puffs 103
Butterscotch Sauce 139
Butterscotch, Sauced 132
Butterscotch Squares 76

Cakes
   An Angel's 9
   Angel Food 19
   Biscuit Shortcake 11
   Black Forest 10
   Blitz Torte 21
   Boston Cream Pie 26
   Carrot 27
   Chocolate Angel 11
   Gingerbread 9
   Orange Angel Dessert 16
   Peach Filled Angel 14
   Peach Shortcake 12
   Peach Upside Down 13
   Pineapple Upside Down 13
   Quick Black Forest 23
   Raspberry Angel Dessert 15
   Raspberry Shortcake 12
   Raspberry Tunnel 11
   Sacher Torte 20
   Strawberry Angel Dessert 15
   Strawberry Shortcake 12
   Strawberry Tunnel 15
   Tunnel Of Peaches 14
Cantaloupe, Fruit Compote 84
Caramel Fruit Dip 86
Carrot Cake 27
Carrot Pudding 111
Chantilly Ginger 25
Chantilly
   Almond 147
   Berry 147
   Brandy 147
   Butterscotch 147
   Chocolate 147

Coffee	147
Cointreau	147
Crème De Menthe	147
Ginger	25
Kahlua	147
Maple	147
Mint	147
Orange	147
Rum	147
Vanilla	147
Cheesecake	31
Cheesecakes	
Best Chocolate	32
Blueberry	30
Cheesecake	31
Cherry	30
Chocolate Swirl	38
Creamy Praline	39
Frozen Mocha	78
Lemon	29
Lemon Chiffon	37
Maple Walnut	39
Praline	39
Pumpkin	34
Raspberry	33
Cherries	
Black Forest Soufflé	50
Chocolate Cherries	146
Quick Black Forest	23
Rainbow Squares	109
Zuccotto	51
Cherries Jubilee	85
Cherry Banana Slice	45
Cherry Cha Cha	69
Cherry Cheesecake	30
Cherry Cobbler	117
Chiffon Cheesecake, Lemon	37
Choco Peanut Butter Topping	140
Chocolate Angel Cake	11
Chocolate Blanc Mange	135
Chocolate Bread Pudding	116
Chocolate Cha Cha	69
Chocolate Chantilly	147
Chocolate Cheesecake, Best	32
Chocolate Cherries	146
Chocolate Coated Mints	145
Chocolate Cottage Pudding	28
Chocolate Crêpes	104
Chocolate Cups	147
Chocolate Custard	133
Chocolate Dipped Fruit	86
Chocolate Dipped Strawberries	86
Chocolate Eclairs	103
Chocolate Fondue	140
Chocolate Ice Cream Roll	80
Chocolate Icing	80
Chocolate Log	80
Chocolate Meringue Torte	94
Chocolate Mints	148
Chocolate Minute Tapioca	120
Chocolate Mousse	62
Chocolate Pie	98
Chocolate Pineapple Dessert	49
Chocolate Pudding Sauce	142
Chocolate Rice Pudding	121
Chocolate Roll	24
Chocolate Sauce, Deluxe	139
Chocolate Sauced Crêpes	104
Chocolate Soufflé	67
Chocolate Spanish Cream	124
Chocolate Swirl Cheesecake	38
Chocolate Tapioca	120
Choux Pastry	
Butterscotch Puffs	103
Chocolate Eclairs	103
Cream Puffs	103
Melba Puffs	103
Profiteroles	103
Cloud Nine	93
Cobblers	117
Coffee	
Irish	149
Monte Cristo	148
Spanish	149
Coffee Caramel	63
Coffee Chantilly	147
Cointreau Chantilly	147
Condensed Milk	137
Confections	
After Dinner Mints	145
Chocolate Cherries	146
Chocolate Coated Mints	145
Chocolate Mints	148
Pecan Bites	145
Truffles	146
Cottage Cheese	
Lemon Chiffon Cheesecake	37
Cottage Pudding	28
Cottage Pudding, Chocolate	28
Crabapple Glaze	96
Cranberry Filling	23
Cranberry Pudding	131
Cream Cheese Filling	25
Cream Cheese Icing	27
Cream Puffs	103
Cream Squares, Danish	41
Creamy Praline Cheesecake	39
Creamy Rice Custard	121
Creamy Rice Pudding	121

Crème Brûlée	112
Crème Caramel	133
Crème De Menthe Chantilly	147
Crêpes	104
Crêpes	
Apricot	104
Black Forest	98
Blueberry	104
Butterscotch	104
Chocolate	104
Chocolate Sauced	104
Strawberry	104
Strawberry Cream	105
Custard	133
Custard Sauce	133
Dacquoise	92
Danish Apple Bars	100
Danish Cream Squares	41
Danish Soufflé	60
Deep Apple	115
Deep Fried Ice Cream	73
Deluxe Chocolate Sauce	139
Dips, See Sauces, Toppings	
Drinks, See Beverages	
Dumplings, Apple	99
Easy Fruit Dip	86
Easy Fruit Sauce	84
Economical Cha Cha	69
English Trifle	130
Filling, Cream Cheese	25
Filling, Lemon	22
Filling, Lemon	95
Fillings, See Sauces, Toppings	
Flapper Pie	102
Fondue	
Chocolate	140
Lemon	141
White	140
Fondue Dippers	140
Fresh Fruit Betty	115
Frosty Clouds	91
Frozen Desserts	
Lemon Meringue	77
Mocha Cheesecake	78
See Ice Cream Desserts	
Strawberry Freeze	74
Frozen Lemon Meringue	77
Frozen Mocha Cheesecake	78
Fruit Caramel	87
Fruit, Chocolate Dipped	86
Fruit Compote	84
Fruit Dips, Toppings	
Caramel Fruit	86
Easy Fruit Dip	86
Easy Fruit Sauce	84
Fruit Dressing	84
Fruit Sauce	85
Fruit Topping	137
Orange Sauce	138
Fruit Dressing	84
Fruit Glazes	
Apple Jelly	96
Apricot	82
Simple	96
Strawberry	96
Fruit Pizza	82
Fruit Sauce	85
Fruit Topping	137
Fruit Topping, See Fruit Dips, Toppings	
Fruit Torte	110
Fruit Tray	86
Fruit Trifle	118
Fudge Pudding, Saucy	128
Ginger, Chantilly	25
Gingerbread	9
Glazes, See Fruit Glazes	
Glorified Rice	62
Grapes, Fruit Compote	84
Hard Sauce	141
Honeydew, Fruit Compote	84
Ice Cream, Deep Fried	73
Ice Cream Desserts	
Apple Alaska Bake	73
Baked Alaska	75
Butterscotch Squares	76
Cherries Jubilee	85
Chocolate Ice Cream Roll . . .	80
Deep Fried Ice Cream	73
Ice Cream Toffee Slice	76
Mocha Baked Alaska	75
Mud Pie	79
Peach Melba	87
Peaches And Ice Cream	81
Pumpkin Ice Cream Pie	70
Watermelon Bombe	76
Ice Cream Filling	22
Ice Cream Toffee Slice	76
Instant Fruit Caramel	87
Instant Lemon Dessert	44
Irish Coffee	149
Jellied Dessert, Quick	63
Jelly Roll	22
Jelly Rolls	
Chocolate	24

Chocolate Ice Cream	80
Chocolate Log	80
Pumpkin	25
Kahlua Chantilly	147
Kiwifruit	
Fruit Compote	84
Fruit Pizza	82
Pavlova	96
Layered Lemon	43
Lemon Cheesecake	29
Lemon Chiffon	122
Lemon Chiffon Cheesecake	37
Lemon Cream Sauce	141
Lemon Dessert, Instant	44
Lemon Filling	22
Lemon Filling	95
Lemon Fondue	141
Lemon Jelly Dessert	48
Lemon, Layered	43
Lemon Meringue, Frozen	77
Lemon Sauce	141
Lemon Sauced Pudding	129
Lemon Snow	47
Lemon Torte	95
Mandarin Oranges,	
Fruit Compote	84
Maple Bavarian	52
Maple Chantilly	147
Maple Walnut Cheesecake	39
Marshmallow Chip Squares	59
Marshmallow Fruit Squares	59
Melba, Peach	87
Melba Puffs	103
Melba Sauce	136
Meringue Desserts	
Apple Alaska Bake	73
Baked Alaska	75
Blitz Torte	21
Bocconne Dolce	97
Chocolate Meringue Torte	94
Chocolate Pie	98
Cloud Nine	93
Dacquoise	92
Frosty Clouds	91
Frozen Lemon	77
Lemon Torte	95
Mocha Baked Alaska	75
Pavlova	96
Queen of Puddings	116
Rice Meringue Pudding	121
Strawberry Meringue	
Shortcake	97
Meringue Shortcake	97
Mince Tarts	110
Mint Chantilly	147
Mint Dessert	61
Mints	
After Dinner	145
Chocolate	148
Chocolate Coated	145
Minute Tapioca	
Chocolate	120
Regular	120
Minute Tapioca Pudding	120
Mocha Baked Alaska	75
Mocha Cha Cha	69
Mocha Cheesecake, Frozen	78
Mocha Sauced Pudding	132
Monte Cristo	148
Mousse, Chocolate	62
Mud Pie	79
Orange Angel Dessert	16
Orange Chantilly	147
Orange Sauce	138
Orange Sauce, Simple	138
Oranges	
Banana Split Dessert	46
Fruit Compote	84
Packaged Milk Puddings	114
Pastry	105
Pavlova	96
Peach Cream	23
Peach Filled Angel Cake	14
Peach Melba	87
Peach Shortcake	12
Peach Upside Down Cake	13
Peaches And Cream	65
Peaches And Ice Cream	81
Peaches, Brandied	88
Pears Hélène	82
Pecan Bites	145
Pie Crust Pastry	105
Pies	
Boston Cream	26
Chocolate	98
Deep Apple	115
Flapper	102
Mince Tarts	110
Mud	79
Praline	113
Pumpkin Ice Cream	70
Pineapple	
Banana Split Dessert	46
Dessert, Chocolate	49
Fruit Compote	84
Pink Lady	42
Rainbow Squares	109
Pineapple Delight	55

Pineapple Sauce	137
Pineapple Upside Down Cake	13
Pink Lady	42
Pistachio Dessert	68
Plum Pudding	123
Praline Cheesecake	39
Praline Pie	113
Profiteroles	103
Pudding Sauce	
Brown Sugar	142
Chocolate	142
Rum	142
Rum Raisin	142
Vanilla	142
Pumpkin Cheesecake	34
Pumpkin Cream Squares	40
Pumpkin Ice Cream Pie	70
Pumpkin Jelly Roll	25
Pumpkin Torte	66
Queen Of Puddings	116
Quick Apple Pudding	127
Quick Black Forest	23
Quick Jellied Dessert	63
Quick Pudding	132
Rainbow Squares	109
Raisin Pudding	111
Raspberry Angel Dessert	15
Raspberry Cheesecake	33
Raspberry Filling	22
Raspberry Mallow Squares	56
Raspberry Sauce, Melba	136
Raspberry Shortcake	12
Raspberry Swirl	64
Raspberry Tunnel	11
Regular Minute Tapioca	120
Rhubarb Betty	115
Rice Meringue Pudding	121
Rice Puddings	
Chocolate	121
Creamy	121
Creamy Custard	121
Glorified	62
Rum Chantilly	147
Rum Hard Sauce	141
Rum Raisin Sauce	142
Rum Sauce	142
Sacher Torte	20
Sauce, See Pudding Sauce	
Sauced Bananas	91
Sauced Butterscotch	132
Sauces, Toppings, Fillings, Dips	
Apricot	139
Blueberry	136
Brandy Hard	141
Brown Sugar	142
Butterscotch	139
Choco Peanut Butter	140
Chocolate Pudding	142
Cranberry	23
Cream Cheese	25
Custard	133
Deluxe Chocolate	139
Easy Fruit	84
Fruit	137
Hard	141
Lemon	22
Lemon	95
Lemon	141
Lemon Cream	141
Melba	136
Orange	138
Peach Cream	23
Pineapple	137
Raspberry	22
Rum	142
Rum Hard	141
Rum Raisin	142
Simple Orange	138
Strawberry	23
Strawberry Cream	23
Vanilla Pudding	142
Saucy Fudge Pudding	128
Seedless Grapes, Fruit Compote	84
Sex in a Pan	
Six Layer Dessert	57
Shortcake	
Biscuit	11
Peach	12
Raspberry	12
Strawberry	12
Strawberry Meringue	97
Self Saucing Puddings	
Lemon Sauced	129
Mocha Sauced	132
Quick	132
Quick Apple	127
Sauced Butterscotch	132
Saucy Fudge	128
Simple Fruit Glaze	96
Simple Orange Sauce	138
Six Layer Dessert	57
Soufflés	
Black Forest	50
Chocolate	67
Danish	60
White	67
Spanish Coffee	149
Spanish Cream	124

Spanish Cream, Chocolate	124
Steamed Ginger Pudding	114
Steamed Puddings	
Carrot	111
Ginger	114
Plum	123
Vanilla	131
Steamed Vanilla Pudding	131
Strawberries	
Berry Torte	106
Bocconne Dolce	97
Chocolate Dipped	86
English Trifle	130
Fruit Compote	84
Fruit Pizza	82
Pavlova	96
Pink Lady	42
Strawberries Romanoff	83
Strawberry Angel Dessert	15
Strawberry Bavarian	44
Strawberry Butterscotch	128
Strawberry Cream	23
Strawberry Cream Crêpes	105
Strawberry Crêpes	104
Strawberry Delight	55
Strawberry Freeze	74
Strawberry Glaze	96
Strawberry Meringue Shortcake	97
Strawberry Sauce	23
Strawberry Shortcake	12
Strawberry Tunnel	15
Sweetened Condensed Milk	137
Swiss Roll, See Jelly Rolls	
Tapioca	
Chocolate	120
Minute	120
Regular	120
Toppings, See Sauces And Toppings	
Trifle	118
Trifle, English	130
Trifle, Fruit	118
Trifle In A Pan	112
Truffles	146
Tunnel of Peaches	14
Vanilla Chantilly	147
Vanilla Pudding Sauce	142
Vanilla Pudding, Steamed	131
Watermelon Bombe	76
Watermelon, Fruit Compote	84
White Fondue	140
White Soufflé	67
Whipped Cream, Chantilly	147
Zuccotto	51

MAIL ORDER FORM

Company's Coming Cookbooks Are Available at Retail Locations Everywhere

Deduct $5.00 for every $35.00 ordered

Save $5.00

COMPANY'S COMING SERIES

ENGLISH

Quantity		Quantity		Quantity	
	150 Delicious Squares		Vegetables		Microwave Cooking
	Casseroles		Main Courses		Preserves
	Muffins & More		Pasta		Light Casseroles
	Salads		Cakes		Chicken, Etc.
	Appetizers		Barbecues		Kids Cooking
	Desserts		Dinners of the World		Fish & Seafood *(NEW)*
	Soups & Sandwiches		Lunches		Breads *(NEW)*
	Holiday Entertaining		Pies		Meatless Cooking (April 1997)
	Cookies		Light Recipes		

NO. OF BOOKS   PRICE

FIRST BOOK: $12.99 + $3.00 shipping = **$15.99 each** x [ ] = $[ ]
ADDITIONAL BOOKS: $12.99 + $1.50 shipping = **$14.49 each** x [ ] = $[ ]

PINT SIZE BOOKS

Quantity		Quantity		Quantity	
	Finger Food		Buffets		Chocolate
	Party Planning		Baking Delights		

NO. OF BOOKS   PRICE

FIRST BOOK: $4.99 + $2.00 shipping = **$6.99 each** x [ ] = $[ ]
ADDITIONAL BOOKS: $4.99 + $1.00 shipping = **$5.99 each** x [ ] = $[ ]

JEAN PARÉ LIVRES DE CUISINE

FRENCH

Quantity		Quantity		Quantity	
	150 délicieux carrés		Délices des fêtes		Les casseroles légères
	Les casseroles		Recettes légères		Poulet, etc.
	Muffins et plus		Les salades		La cuisine pour les enfants
	Les dîners		La cuisson au micro-ondes		Poissons et fruits de mer
	Les barbecues		Les pâtes		Les pains *(NEW)*
	Les tartes		Les conserves		La cuisine sans viande (avril 1997) *(NEW)*

NO. OF BOOKS   PRICE

FIRST BOOK: $12.99 + $3.00 shipping = **$15.99 each** x [ ] = $[ ]
ADDITIONAL BOOKS: $12.99 + $1.50 shipping = **$14.49 each** x [ ] = $[ ]

TOTAL

- MAKE CHEQUE OR MONEY ORDER PAYABLE TO: *COMPANY'S COMING PUBLISHING LIMITED*
- ORDERS OUTSIDE CANADA: Must be paid in U.S. funds by cheque or money order drawn on Canadian or U.S. bank.
- Prices subject to change without prior notice.
- Sorry, no C.O.D.'s

TOTAL PRICE FOR ALL BOOKS $[ ]
Less $5.00 for every $35.00 ordered − $[ ]
SUBTOTAL $[ ]
Canadian residents add G.S.T. + $[ ]
TOTAL AMOUNT ENCLOSED $[ ]

Please complete shipping address on reverse.

Gift Giving

- Let us help you with your gift giving!
- We will send cookbooks directly to the recipients of your choice if you give us their names and addresses.
- Be sure to specify the titles you wish to send to each person.
- If you would like to include your personal note or card, we will be pleased to enclose it with your gift order.
- Company's Coming Cookbooks make excellent gifts. Birthdays, bridal showers, Mother's Day, Father's Day, graduation or any occasion... collect them all!

Shipping address

Send the Company's Coming Cookbooks listed on the reverse side of this coupon, to:

Name: _____

Street: _____

City: _____ Province/State: _____

Postal Code/Zip: _____ Tel: (_____) _____ — _____

Company's Coming Publishing Limited
Box 8037, Station F
Edmonton, Alberta, Canada T6H 4N9
Tel: (403) 450-6223
Fax: (403) 450-1857

Available April 1997

Cookmark

MEATLESS COOKING

 **COOKBOOKS**

New and Imaginative Ways
to cook up meals your family will love!

- Appetizers, Dips
- Casseroles, Stews
- Desserts
- Pasta, Pizza
- Pies, Quiches
- Sandwiches, Burgers
- Soups, Salads
- Vegetables

Quick & Easy Recipes

Everyday Ingredients

OVER 10 MILLION SOLD IN SERIES

Mark your favorite recipe with this handy tear out **COOKMARK**

Cookmark

Complete your collection.

Look for these *Best-Sellers* where you shop!

COMPANY'S COMING SERIES
Suggested Retail $12.99 each

- ☐ 150 DELICIOUS SQUARES
- ☐ CASSEROLES
- ☐ MUFFINS & MORE
- ☐ SALADS
- ☐ APPETIZERS
- ☐ DESSERTS
- ☐ SOUPS & SANDWICHES
- ☐ HOLIDAY ENTERTAINING
- ☐ COOKIES
- ☐ VEGETABLES
- ☐ MAIN COURSES
- ☐ PASTA
- ☐ CAKES
- ☐ BARBECUES
- ☐ DINNERS OF THE WORLD
- ☐ LUNCHES
- ☐ PIES
- ☐ LIGHT RECIPES
- ☐ MICROWAVE COOKING
- ☐ PRESERVES
- ☐ LIGHT CASSEROLES
- ☐ CHICKEN, ETC.
- ☐ KIDS COOKING
- ☐ FISH & SEAFOOD
- ☐ BREADS
- ☐ MEATLESS COOKING (April 1997)

PINT SIZE BOOKS
Suggested Retail $4.99 each

- ☐ FINGER FOOD
- ☐ PARTY PLANNING
- ☐ BUFFETS
- ☐ BAKING DELIGHTS
- ☐ CHOCOLATE

All New Recipes

Sample Recipe from Meatless Cooking

ZUCCHINI CUTLETS

So colorful with red and green showing throughout. A wonderful addition to a meal.

Finely grated carrot	½ cup	125 mL
Chopped onion	½ cup	125 mL
Chopped red pepper	¼ cup	60 mL
Chopped green pepper	¼ cup	60 mL
Fine soda cracker crumbs	2 cups	500 mL
All-purpose flour	¼ cup	60 mL
Baking powder	1 tsp.	5 mL
Salt	¾ tsp.	4 mL
Pepper	⅛ tsp.	0.5 mL
Grated zucchini, with peel	3 cups	750 mL
Large eggs, lightly beaten	2	2
Cooking oil	2 tbsp.	30 mL

Measure first 9 ingredients into bowl. Stir.

Mix in zucchini and eggs. Shape into cutlets (patties) using about ¼ cup (60 mL) for each.

Heat cooking oil in frying pan. Brown cutlets on both sides. Makes about 1 dozen.

Variation: For more protein add grated cheese.

Use this handy checklist to complete your collection of **Company's Coming Cookbooks**